PHOTOGRAPH OF TOMMY ARMOUR BY HANK COHEN

HOW TO PLAY
Your Best Golf
ALL THE TIME

TOMMY ARMOUR

ILLUSTRATED BY LEALAND GUSTAVSON

A FIRESIDE BOOK
Published by Simon & Schuster
New York London Toronto Sydney Tokyo Singapore

With my esteem and gratitude this book is dedicated to the ever-aspiring golfers. The Lord must love them—He made so many of them.

TOMMY ARMOUR

FIRESIDE
Rockefeller Center
1230 Avenue of the Americas
New York, New York 10020

FIRESIDE and colophon are registered trademarks
of Simon & Schuster Inc.

Manufactured in the United States of America

10 9 8 7 6 5 4 3 2

Library of Congress Cataloging-in-Publication Data is available.

ISBN 0-684-81379-3

CONTENTS

CHAPTER ONE

Why This Book Is as Short and Simple as It Is

AFTER declining numerous proposals to write a book of golf instruction, I took on the task which this book represents.

The responsibility was accepted because I have been allowed to teach in this book as I teach on the lesson tee — without embellishment or padding to stretch out the basic training, and without a multitude of detail to confuse the pupil.

The brevity of this book may shock those who have been encouraged to believe that a good golf game may be bought by the page, pound or hour — or even bought.

I have paid for hundreds of lessons when I was a lad and didn't have much money to pay as tuition fees. Vardon, Duncan, Braid, Taylor and Edgar — all great players and all gifted teachers — were among my instructors who not only taught me the foundation of golf but also taught me how to learn.

Association with the greatest American players added to my instruction. As I competed against them I studied them, and as I have played friendly rounds with them or followed them in some of their competitions, I have continued to be the student.

Simplicity, concentration, and economy of time and effort have been the distinguishing features of the great players' and great teachers' methods which have added to what I consider my knowledge of the game.

Hundreds of pages that might have accompanied these that you will read were eliminated from the first draft of the manuscript. Dozens of illustrations showing interim phases of the swing were cut out, and I have retained only those pictorial moments in the swing which are significant in so far as instruction is concerned. I decided that those pages and drawings portrayed refinements of technique not suitable for the practical use of most golfers and would distract the reader from profitable concentration on the essentials.

CHAPTER TWO

How To Learn Your Best Golf

WHILE trimming my manuscript down to the form in which it now reaches you, I often thought of men and women who might have been great champions had they only been able to master the simple and indispensable elements of good golf I have set forth in this book. The frustrated ones lost their way to glory by wandering in a maze of detail.

That never has happened to any of my pupils, and it never will, whether the pupil is a beginner or one who already has won national championships.

Instead of being on my lesson tee you are reading my book. That puts me at a disadvantage in my endeavor to teach you the best golf within your capabilities. The most effective instruction obviously calls for a partnership of pupil and tutor that is best achieved by close personal association. But somewhat to my surprise, and certainly to my gratification, I think I've come pretty close to doing my share on these printed pages. The rest will be up to you.

There has been criticism that some professional golfers do not know how to teach. In defense of my competent colleagues in professional golf, I must point out that many golf pupils don't know how to take a lesson.

Let's have a bit of instruction on that matter, now.

In the first place, you won't be able to finish reading this book and go out and cut fifteen strokes off your game the next time you play. But where you will be advanced the next time you play is in knowing, very definitely, some things you must do to produce an improved score.

Understand that this is not a book about a soft way to great golf.

Anyone who tells you there is such a way is lying or doesn't know golf.

This book that is bringing you and me together requires that the reader use some brains. If you are not prepared to do that, let's call it off here. I never have wasted my time on anyone who wants to play good golf but who either hasn't any gray matter or won't use it. And I won't begin now. I prize my performance and reputation as a helpful teacher far too much to risk it on the lazy-minded.

My contributions to the very satisfactory progress of pupils have been made primarily on the policy of sound simplicity. This gives results.

Your golf must — and will — be improved when you realize that our objective is to get a complex mortal to simplify the positions and actions in good golf as much as possible.

I'll tell you how, but I can't do it for you.

Possibly you have been made a victim of the great delusion in golf, that of believing the answer lies in tricks rather than in mastery of the alphabet of golfing knowledge. I will have no part of catering to that fond and fantastic dream of the gullible.

But, to get into the effective application of the instruction in this book:

There are simple and certain key positions and actions that I have indicated by having them printed **in red** in the following pages. The sentences and paragraphs thus indicated are especially significant in the evolution of the soundest golf the reader's physical and temperamental qualifications permit. In other words — they are the keys to *How To Play Your Best Golf All the Time.*

This book is, frankly, a textbook and as such requires intelligent study if the reader is going to pass the examination on the golf course.

It is a book to be studied with a golf club alongside you, so you can pause while you are reading, take the club and work out the point that the text is covering.

In that way you translate the type and the illustrations into a language your muscles can read and remember.

In that way, and in that way alone, can you coordinate thinking and action under circumstances that let the lesson sink in deep enough to stay with you. Otherwise, when you next get on a golf course and need exactly what I've told you in this book, at that time you will have your attention split between your eagerness to make a shot and your effort to remember what I told you to do.

Then is when your muscles should be helping you to remember instructions. But if you haven't given them a chance to study with you as you read, they're not of much assistance to you.

What you should do as you study this book is exactly what I have my pupils do on the lesson tee; take an 8-iron and let your muscles and your brains learn together.

I will put before you in this book, as concisely and clearly as possible, what you must do to get a solid foundation for the best golf you can play. After all the playing and teaching I've done, I've taken a club and stood before a mirror and again reviewed and studied certain positions and actions. I wanted to make absolutely certain that I was describing them in a way that you would be sure to comprehend them completely.

This was done to make certain that in print you would get exactly what my personal pupils get even though I can't look at you while you are applying the lesson.

Apply your study as you read and don't wait until you get outside.

The shaft of the 8-iron is short enough so, with due regard for the walls, ceiling, furniture and flooring, you can physically check up on what your mentality is absorbing.

Put a magazine on the floor so if the clubhead does make contact no damage will be done. If you want to use the soft synthetic rubber, knit, or felt practice balls for your study of some phases of the instruction, they're O.K. for use on the protective surface you've got over your flooring or floor covering, but practice balls aren't essential. Some find them helpful; others don't. It's apparently a matter of temperament.

But the big point is to make a habit of applying the positions and the actions as you study. By doing that you get the feeling, and you can see, with thorough understanding, what you must do.

I never try to teach by telling what NOT to do. My job is to teach you what to do. You probably will do plenty of things wrong without any warnings from me which might suggest them to you. Most players are unfortunately inclined to make golf more complicated than this theoretically simple sport actually is.

Study with your brains and muscles the positive way. Take your time and get the details right. I have reduced the details to the utmost practical minimum.

As you study your positions and your movements, make sure that they check absolutely with the points indicated in the illustrations.

I've observed that almost all aspiring golfers fail to see the real story told in action photographs of expert golfers. So I have decided to have the illustrations in this book be line drawings, with details accurately and sharply brought into focus, and explained in type. This may not be as pretty as a photograph, but it will be more readily understood and assimilated.

When a high-speed camera takes pictures of a golfer making a shot, it's customary in most golf instruction books to break the action into each split second of the swing. Anything from perhaps fifteen to thirty separate phases of the complete shot are shown for every club

Address   Top of the Swing

from the driver down to the No. 9. Now all you need is a little multiplication to show you how many hundreds of photographs you can have in a golf book. They may be interesting to look at, but my instruction technique is to teach you *a few things to do right,* and from that standpoint such a great number of pictures is meaningless and confusing.

Here are the ones which matter — the *only* positions necessary to study and get right. (I have used the fairway wood shot for illustration purposes.)

Entering the Hitting Area   Impact

9

That gives you only four illustrations to study in a swing, and at each point there are definite things which should be right at that point, as I'll explain more fully later on in this book. If those things are right, everything else in between and following must fit in the right way, too.

For example, you may find to your horror that I never mention or picture the complete follow-through, except in discussing bunker shots. That means I've left out some very graceful and eye-catching pictures I could have used in this book. But I'm convinced that any emphasis on the follow-through in golf instruction is just one more thing for the pupil to remember, and one which won't help him. There are two reasons for this. First, if the ball is hit correctly, it's on its way anyhow, and it doesn't matter how you follow through, and if it has been hit correctly you are bound to follow through — naturally. Secondly, it's a peculiar thing but the people who concentrate specifically on following through are often the very ones who quit on a shot in the actual hitting area.

So, since I am trying to teach you golf in this book, I haven't tried to confuse the issue by dressing it up with either text or illustrations which don't matter. Only the most experienced professionals know how to "read" action pictures of experts, but I am convinced that the manner in which the drawings in this book are presented will not only help teach you now, but will also establish a basis for your study of golf photographs in the future.

The inspection of the individual characteristics and general features of expert players is often of benefit to the average player, once he knows what's important.

Now I believe you have solid groundwork for your study, understanding, and use of this book. Think and act about the text and illustrations as I have advised you to do. Then you will come as near as any absentee possibly can to getting the benefit of my personal instruction at the Boca Raton lesson tee. Incidentally, the charge will be several hundred dollars less than that paid by those with whom I share the mutually responsible and pleasantly rewarding relationship of golf instructor and student.

CHAPTER THREE

What Can Your Best Golf Be?

A DISCOVERY I've made as a contestant, observer, and student at innumerable professional and amateur golf championships is a simple fact that undoubtedly will improve your scoring. Here it is:

It is not solely the capacity to make great shots that makes champions, but the essential quality of making very few bad shots.

Watch at the practice tee of any major tournament and you will see many players hit a very high percentage of perfect shots with every club in the bag. Then watch them as they play. They will make superb shots, but they will make too many bad ones.

Their bad shots may be because of faulty execution or the less pardonable reason of bad judgment. But regardless of the cause, they've exceeded the limit of allowable error. In major championship golf the margin of error is narrow. It's wide in the club competitions between higher handicap players, but there, as well as in expert competitions, you'll note that what distinguishes the winner is that he made fewer bad strokes than the rest.

The champion is the fellow who can make the fewest poor shots. What first vividly impressed me with that fact was an experience I had with Walter Hagen.

Walter and I were playing the final round of a North and South Open. I was leading the field when that fourth round started at Pinehurst. I played the first three holes of that round 4-4-3. Hagen had begun 6-6-5.

As we walked to the fourth tee, Hagen in his high drawl said to me: "I've missed all I can spare today; now I'm going to work."

He went to work — and on me.

He didn't miss any more shots that round.

He rubbed out my lead, finished with a 68, and won the tournament.

That lesson cost me plenty, but although I fancied myself as a very keen scholar of golf, I hadn't known what I learned then. That was when I discovered the secret that the way to win was by making fewer bad shots.

Now let's go from that lesson to an application I made of it at Boca Raton. Among my pupils there is a prominent steel man. In lessons and in practice he hits many excellent shots. He's a good hitter but a bad player.

In a moment of high confidence in the grill room, he expressed his conviction that he could break 90. There were numerous differences of opinion. The outcome was as is customary when there are differences of opinion regarding sports events.

It was agreed that as I had risked a bold wager in

support of my pupil, I could accompany him as counselor during the round.

He hit a long, strong drive off the first tee, but in the rough, to the right.

He walked up to make his second shot and picked out a 5-iron to go for the green.

"Put that back in the bag," I told him.

"I've got a chance to go for a birdie," he protested.

"You've got a bigger chance of missing the shot, then having another tough one to make before you get on," I explained. "Play an easy 8-iron shot out to the left to where you have another easy shot through the opening of the green. Then you may get yourself a one-putt par."

So that's the way he played the hole, and that's the way it showed on the card . . . par 4.

To his and my amazement and delight — and profit — he went around in 79.

Hole after hole I'd had to argue with him and explain to him that there are two sound rules for low scoring that apply in nine hundred ninety-nine out of a thousand cases.

These rules — or practical principles, are:

Play the shot you've got the greatest chance of playing well, and

Play the shot that makes the next shot easy.

If it's mystified you to see fellows with worse swings

than yours score better than you do, the mystery will be cleared if you'll note how, instinctively, or by deliberately using their heads, they've applied the two tactical principles I've just set before you.

When you get that lesson in your head, you will greatly improve your scoring. There are plenty of other lessons about making golf shots and we'll get to them in due time in this book, but the main lesson about playing golf is the one I've just given you.

There are variations of this lesson in playing. The variations are determined by match and stroke play and by the player's proficiency. The expert can take more chances with less risk than can the average or high handicap golfer.

Some never learn to play the type of game that fits their capabilities. Countless times I've seen ordinary players try to play courses in ways that would require the shot-making techniques of the most highly gifted stars. Such players may know something about grip, stance and swing, but they don't know the first thing about playing golf.

That mistake isn't made by the champions. Walter Travis knew his weak points. He couldn't get much distance. And he also knew that he was superior in accuracy and in the short game. His winning tactics were to fit his game to the course he was playing.

Lawson Little was an excellent shot-maker before I ever saw him, but he wasn't winning as he should. About all I taught him was tactics. When he learned tactics, he won four American and British national amateur championships in two consecutive years, and later won the American National Open title and other events against fine professional fields.

Julius Boros was a very good shot-maker before he started winning major events. He wasn't winning because he didn't have a tactical plan of play that fitted his game. He was playing in a cautious way that fitted neither his ability nor his temperament.

I suggested to him that since he was one of the best I'd ever seen in playing out of traps, he could change from his plan of trying to steer shots and boldly let them fly. Then if a shot came to rest in a trap around a green he had nothing to worry about, as he could come out close enough to the cup to sink his putt.

He had been unnaturally cautious as a putter. When it was impressed upon him that he very, very rarely missed much to either side of the cup but often failed to get up to the hole with putts that were precisely on the line, he began putting with more confidence and by daring to get the ball to the hole, or even past, improved his putting.

Boros is a strong player who'd been trying to play with a tightening fear of being wild with his long shots. When he learned to swing freely rather than steer in making his long shots and to depend on the precision of his short game, he became a champion.

Every golfer scores better when he learns his capabilities.

This is the first time I've ever mentioned what I am certain is my greatest value to my pupils. I learn about them before I try to teach them. I determine, pretty closely, what is the best golf each individual can possibly play.

It is utterly illogical to expect a person with physical, temperamental, and manner-of-living limitations to become able to play par or sub-par championship golf. One might as well expect to become a great master of painting, sculpture, the violin or piano, become a scientific genius, or even to become rich, simply by taking lessons and practicing.

I've taught some of the greatest golfers a few of the polishing details that have helped them get as near to perfection as is possible. That has been comparatively easy because they have an aptitude for learning, sound basic ability, and fine physical qualifications. But the utmost demands on my own capabilities as an instructor have been made by those who are shooting the courses in 85 or up into three figures, discovering what would be their best games and teaching them to perform consistently to the limit of their capacities.

Golf is a comparative game. That is the marvelous merit of golf's handicapping system.

Ellsworth Vines pointed out this attraction of golf

when he told me that in tennis, when he was starring, there were less than a dozen who could give him an exciting and entertaining game, but in golf he could get a fine, close match with a dub or an expert because of the handicapping.

Certainly a game that permits many thousands all over the United States to play against champions, with the handicaps making all contestants equal at the start, has a feature of enjoyment that makes it unique.

At Boca Raton, in the winter, and at northern courses in the spring, summer and fall, I play many rounds with players whose average scores range from 85 to 110, and we have very close games on the handicaps.

You might think I'd be bored playing with a real duffer, but I don't find that to be the case. In the first place he interests me by being so bad when he might well be so much better. He will hit some excellent shots, but they're hit by accident and I wonder how I might make such accidents become consistent.

The principal error in viewpoint of a majority of golfers is failure to understand that if they play to a uniform standard that is well within their capabilities, the handicapping system will take care of the rest. They'll probably take money from many proficient professionals and amateurs to whom the handicaps allow an extremely small margin of error.

But they all want to be stars when they just simply haven't got it in them. As the Bard might have said,

"Ambition is a grievous fault and grievously doth the duffer pay."

You see overvaulting ambition at its dirty work when the 95-shooter gets an 82 with twenty-five putts and ten lucky bounces. He thinks he is an 82 performer, whereas he actually has a game of about 87 under best normal circumstances. If he has once shot an 82, he rarely realizes that in scoring 87, considering his limitations, he's doing as well comparatively as the gifted player who goes around in 68.

The most difficult part of my responsibility as a teacher is to determine what is the best my pupil could consistently score. Then I can teach him to do that. If he shows unexpected promise after reaching that goal, we can advance together toward the next higher plateau of learning.

Heaven knows I want every pupil to become as good as is humanly possible, but the more realistic part of my work is to make reasonably certain that he never gets more than a few strokes worse than he should be.

The fact that at least ninety per cent of the millions of golfers score in the 90's — or approximately a stroke a hole over par — is highly significant. It is a plain indication of their inherent limitations. Few of them are reconciled to their limitations. Fortunately, practically all of them can learn to reduce many of the faults that are preventing them from getting as close to par as nature will allow them.

But they must be willing to learn.

There are at least six people who want to be taught golf to every one who wants to learn.

My task with those six is to make them understand primarily their attainable objective, the rational method of achieving their aim, and the relationship that must exist during a lesson.

The very best I can do for them — or for anybody else — is to get them started correctly on the most solid and lasting basis of improvement; a basis on which they establish the best game they ultimately can play.

To bring you as close as possible to my lesson tee at Boca Raton so you can see the personal application of what I must get into your mind and muscle with type and illustration in this book, I'll tell you how I give a lesson.

CHAPTER FOUR

Taking You to the Lesson Tee

WHAT MOST golf pupils want is the maximum of improvement with the minimum of exertion. I can't blame them for that. Golf to them is to be a delightful relaxation and escape from work rather than work in another guise.

So I start the lesson by making clear to them that we are not engaged in a matter of life or death but in a pleasant, intriguing venture that has as its obvious objective the hitting of a ball.

If they don't hit the ball as they should, that need not embarrass them; if they don't hit it after I've been trying to teach them, I'm the one to be embarrassed.

I want them to start in without any fear at all. Fear ruins more golf shots, for duffer and star, than any other one factor.

I never begin from a cold start. Each pupil has to warm up in thinking and attitude, just as the star does before a tournament round.

Perhaps you have wondered why I didn't start off this book telling you how to hold the club, or with some other technical information. I didn't because I want to come as near as I can to giving you in this book the sort of a lesson I give on the tee. I want to condition the mentality of the pupil to the lesson and protect him against the danger of impatiently rushing at a task he doesn't adequately understand.

Action before thought is the ruination of most of your shots.

It stands to reason you must know what to think about before you step up to hit the ball.

So the first step in my lesson is to have a chat with the pupil, during which I develop a clear understanding that the first thing I must do for him is to get him in the receptive condition for learning. I'll attend to the teaching.

By the way, while I refer to the pupil as "him," many of my pupils are girls and women. In fact, some of the most satisfactory, most quickly developing pupils I've taught are those of the gentler sex.

What often enables them to advance possibly a little faster than men is that seldom do they want to do the teaching. There are a number of men who are so full of golf theories, tips and hunches, they seem to have a burning desire to teach me instead of learning.

There is basically no difference between men's and women's golf. Women's golf is simply a smaller edition of the men's game.

I suspect that today's crowded golf courses somewhat

delay progress in women's scoring by not providing encouraging practice opportunities.

Women are usually more inclined to accept and respond to instruction than men are. Some men are disposed to think that they have great innate athletic ability and it should be easy for the teaching professional to expose and adapt to golf this vast hidden talent. The truth may be that the man is inherently clumsy and never was the athlete he thinks he was, or due to his sedentary work he's badly out of responsive physical condition.

I see no reason for believing that women will become superior to men at golf, any more than one can expect women to outclass men at tennis, baseball, softball, or bowling.

But, again, I remind you that golf is comparative and on that basis the women can boast that the average of their golf has improved at a more rapid rate than that of men's scoring.

Necessity compelled an arrangement that gives my pupils a properly balanced diet of instruction and practice, and it turned out to be a good idea. Due to the crowded pages of my lesson calendar, I must limit each pupil to no more than three lessons a week.

Therefore, I tell the pupil to devote the interim between lessons to practice. I soon found that, unless it was evident that my pupil actually had absorbed a previous lesson by practicing on it before the next lesson was due, he wasn't a pupil who was going to get very far. In such cases I often suggest that we call off the whole thing.

This may seem to be pretty much of a high-handed procedure, but it has the absolutely valid excuse of there being more pupils than there is time available for them. And, if memory serves me, the pupil at school who didn't attend to his homework — the equivalent of golf practice — ran more of a risk of being flunked out of class. The same idea applied itself to my teaching, and although I didn't adopt the idea deliberately, it works to the benefit of all the pupils who really want to learn. I tell you about it here to re-emphasize my point that I can teach you things, but you have to practice them in order to do them consistently.

I teach only in the mornings; usually each morning except Sunday during the winter season. The pupil is fresher and in better condition to absorb and react properly in the morning, and all-day teaching would be too tiring for me.

In the afternoon I play golf for relaxation, and, in an instructional vein, incidentally use my own game to teach my playing companions how to play intelligent golf without tension.

Too many golfers want to fight the course. I show them how to be in most effective playing condition physically and mentally by disciplining their thinking and meeting the course problems so they'll have the minimum number of difficult and discouraging shots to play.

In a general way my mornings are devoted to teaching my pupils to play shots, and my afternoons to training them to play golf.

All golf is divided into three parts: the strokes, the course, and the opponent.

I can teach the first two parts. I know the third part, but I don't know, or never have known, anyone who could teach it. A great deal of it consists of shooting the heart out of the opposition by playing, in critical situations, shots better than you could make normally — sometimes shots better than you really know how to make.

The set-up for my golf instruction has been commented on as somewhat on the Hollywood style of stage management, although it's an affair of cold, calculated, practical psychology and the most effective pedagogy I can devise.

Many of my pupils are men and women of high fame in business, the professions, society, the theater and pictures, and in other sports as well as golf.

To attain and maintain the correct psychological atmosphere, I must make them aware consciously and subconsciously that in my field of endeavor I'm ranked as high, or higher, than they are in their work, and during this particular hour, I am in command, because by far the greater part of the responsibility is mine.

My teaching lessons all are an hour long. The division of the hour between the physical and mental phases of instruction varies according to the problems and the temperaments of the pupils.

I never give a pupil instruction on irons and on driving the same day.

Driving is hitting the ball off into space. The iron shots must be hit with the true music of crisp, accurate contact of club and ball and have the thrilling result of flying the ball on the beam toward the pin.

The drive is hit slightly on the upswing.

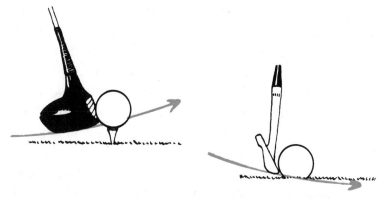

The irons must be hit on the downswing.

To protect my pupils completely against confusion about the two types of shot, I separate the lessons.

There is no part of my teaching on the lesson tee or in this book that is haphazard. The instruction is arranged according to a system that must get one point at a time clearly understood and deeply implanted.

An example of this policy of staying with the subject involves one of the most famous women players. For two weeks during one period in my instruction to her, she was kept on the 6-, 7-, and 8-irons. She is regarded as the finest iron player women's golf has presented, and she most certainly would not have attained that distinction by a haphazard arrangement of teaching and learning.

After my pupil and I have had our preliminary chat and I get a tip on the golf I.Q., attitude and requirements of the pupil, I have him hit twenty shots with an 8-iron.

From this beginning I can see what the pupil is going to be able to do best and what I'll have to work on most.

I study the pupil's physical qualifications; whether he is strong enough, moves gracefully, and has enough coordination to justify an objective of considerable development, or whether the problem is going to be that of making the most of limited assets.

I sit under the sun umbrella on the tee and think for my pupil and myself while an assistant tees the balls. New balls are used for the lessons. The pupil is subconsciously reminded that nothing is too good for the job at hand.

I never watch the flight of the ball. During the summer my assistant is a professional at a good club. Among the many essentials that he knows is how to tee a ball correctly, and strangely enough this apparently simple and foolproof detail is one about which an amazingly large number of golfers are woefully ignorant.

My assistant signals to me the flight of the ball the pupil hits.

I can tell by having watched the pupil vigilantly why the ball went as it did.

The 8-iron is used as the barometer in order to do away with the pupil's fear of not being able to get the ball into the air. The embarrassment of topping shots brings up a problem of tension, and it is unnecessary to contend with that until after the pupil has acquired some confidence and understanding of what he's expected to do. With an 8-iron, a pupil gets the ball off the ground.

Furthermore the 8-iron is the most constructive, as well as most instructive, club in the bag. The player who can use an 8-iron correctly hasn't much trouble in learning the use of any of the other clubs. With the obvious exception of the putter, the 8-iron should be the most used club in the majority of rounds of golf, whether it's the duffer or the expert who is playing.

You can partially miss a driver shot, a long wood or a long iron, and recover, but if you miss an 8-iron shot you've lost a stroke.

I've found that after teaching the importance of the 8-iron and its correct use, about eighty per cent of my teaching troubles are gone.

Teaching the short irons first not only gives instruction in several vital details common to all shots, but gives the pupil a vital foundation of confidence.

I've already mentioned the tremendous influence of fear in golf. When an average player has a pitch shot over a bunker, he is petrified. He tightens and his concentration and coordination are lost. His fear of the ball going into the sand outweighs and overpowers whatever conception he may have of how to play the shot.

The expert player only sees the bunker at first inspection. Then it vanishes from his mind because he knows how to play the shot which is not a particularly difficult one. He makes the shot with calm and complete assurance.

There is no other game in which dread of results plays as important and as frequent a part as in golf. Hence I establish self-reliance early by introducing the pupil to shot-making technique that requires precision rather than a combination of precision and power.

This cuts in half the basic problem of developing the pupil's faith in himself.

The average golfer can't deliberately hit a long iron or wood properly to save his life. When he does hit such a shot that comes off without flubbing, he doesn't know how he did it.

Knowing from years of experience how comparatively easy it is to teach and to learn the long clubs after the short irons are brought under control, I insist that basic training be with the short irons.

The first four of any series of six lessons I give are with shorter irons, from the 9-iron up to the 5-iron.

All good golfers are strong in the hands and forearms. Their golfing muscles have been developed by a great deal of playing and exercise. The average golfer hasn't much muscular development where he needs it to control the club in fast-moving, powerful action.

Consequently when the expert golfer says, "Don't hold the club too firmly," that's misleading to the average player who interprets the advice to mean holding the club too loosely. What feels like a very easy grip to the skilled player, is equivalent to a hold of quite some intensity to the high handicap player.

Therefore, it's perfectly logical that the high handicap player should engage in some forearm- and finger-strengthening exercises. The simple one of squeezing a tennis ball is quite helpful. Such exercising is a problem for the pupil to solve, rather than the instructor. I can urge these grip exercises, but I can't do them for the pupil, and I know that the pupils may start but probably won't persist in the work, so I have to try to figure out ways of minimizing the danger of their weakness.

The truly great golfer, like the truly great athelete in other sports, is the one who, first, has ability. Second to ability, he has the type of intelligence that fits his sport. And third among the great champion's qualifications is the capacity of taking bad breaks without being upset.

The average golfer is not gifted in those three respects, and despite the probability of his never becoming a star on any of the three counts, he can at least get somewhere nearer the great one by overcoming what is, bluntly, his ignorance.

About ninety per cent of my pupils arrive for instruction in utter confusion.

That's not their fault. There's very little science knows about the joint working of the mind and muscles.

In applying what is known, I have them rest physically after the first twenty balls are hit, and we talk over the situation so they understand our aim.

Then they hit more balls, after which we have another session of explanation and understanding. Seldom does one of my pupils hit as many as eighty balls during an hour's lesson even though the pupil is advanced to the degree I am certain that he is thinking his shots as well as muscling them.

I emphasize cultivation of the positive mental attitude; that helps the pupil to help teach himself. When he has been taught to think clearly about his shot-making and his game, he won't get out on the course and make the mistake of hitting bad shots and excusing himself by believing that he did exactly as I told him.

When he hits a bad shot, he is NOT doing exactly as I told him, so I must get him into the habit of remembering exactly what I did tell him to do and why I told him.

The Thou Shalt Nots of the Holy Writ are the great example of teaching in the negative manner, but the emphatic Thou Shalts get results in golf.

When you miss a shot, never think of what you did wrong. Come up to the next shot thinking of what you must do right.

It's far easier to give you this good advice than to get you to heed it. Despite my constant reminders of the positive in teaching, I have pupils asking, "What did I do wrong?"

Although the error may be obvious, I reply, "I don't know, but I know what you didn't do right," then refer to one of the fairly small number of essentials that was not given proper attention during the shot-making.

The average player misleads and confuses himself trying to think of what he might have done wrong, and not very often does chance play upon the correct explanation of what he should have done right.

By keeping the right way always in sharp focus, I protect pupils against becoming depressed from thinking about a bad shot. It's infinitely better for their game and their personalities to have them cheerfully and in a knowing attitude face the problem of making the next shot properly.

Everything in a lesson I teach is pointed toward inculcating beneficial habits. The pupils have to think consciously at first while making a stroke, but eventually they get into the habit of doing their thinking before they swing at the ball.

Conscious effort of any sort can mean a dangerous interference with the perfection of the stroke if that thinking is attempted while the stroke is being made. The stroke is made faster than deliberate mental processes can function on muscles, hence it is scientifically plain that you can't think about any more than one detail while you are hitting a golf ball.

The big job that you have as a player is to forget everything but hitting the ball as it should be hit. The fewer details that intrude upon your mind as you're swinging, the better. It's the minor details, not the few essentials, that tangle up your swing.

The exceedingly valuable factor of concentration, to which you may have heard great players referring, is simply the capacity of eliminating and keeping out all disturbing details.

Make up your mind before your backswing starts, then let your muscles do the work.

Now you have been told about what would take place if you were on the lesson tee with me at Boca Raton.

This part of the course of instruction is intended to

inspire you to practice with profitably studious application to *practice*, instead of merely to hit shots. That will train your muscles to do their job when you play. Your mind will then be free to help you think your way around the golf course in fewer strokes.

CHAPTER FIVE

How Your Clubs Can Help You

A PUPIL must be equipped properly.

I've had some of the world's richest businessmen come for lessons, and after I've looked them over for their physical qualifications and defects and have seen them hit a few balls, I have stopped them.

The clubs they bought were the best that could be bought — but for somebody else, not them.

The value of their time and the value of the time and thought I have to devote to improving their golf (and for which they're paying me) would make the purchase of correctly fitted equipment the cheapest part of their investment.

Properly fitted clubs are the only part of improved golf that anyone can buy.

There is no national champion, no player making a profit in the precarious occupation of tournament golf, who ever could come close to championship play if his clubs were as ill-fitted as those of many thousands of golfers. Yet it is a serious fact that players who have need of every bit of help in scoring often are hopelessly handicapped by their clubs.

Particularly is this inexcusably true of older players whose swings have been insidiously changed by the years yet who are playing with clubs that constitute an unnecessary handicap.

I've heard attributed to Winston Churchill the statement, said to have been made after his first game of golf, that golf was a game devised by the devil to be played with implements ill-adapted to the purpose.

And I dare say that if he played his first game with any set of clubs that happened to be handy, there was ample justification for the latter part of his judgment.

The Delphic "Know thyself" can be expanded for the golfer with other essential advice: "Know your clubs."

Consider the function that the golf club must perform.

The clubface must travel, between address and the finish of the swing, a distance of twenty to twenty-six feet. Compare that with the short distance between your eye and the sight on a gun barrel. Also bear in mind that about one square inch of the clubface must be in precise contact with one — and only one — sector of a sphere one and sixty-eight hundredths inches in diameter.

While trying to effect this contact, your body is twisting and turning, your feet and legs are moving, your shoulders are turning, your arms are swinging, your wrists are hinging, your fingers are active, and your head is moving probably more than it should be.

All these motions must be coordinated with perfect timing to hit the ball properly.

The aim of these and kindred actions is to get the ball into a hole four and one-quarter inches in diameter that is a considerable distance away.

Now it must be obvious why this task demands that you simplify it as much as possible with implements correctly suited to you.

No other game is as exacting as golf in that so many specifications must be met to make a precision fit of implement and player.

Consequently, infinite pains, considerable genius, and fortunes in money are devoted to club design and construction to produce clubs that will make golf easier. As long as the fundamental character of the game isn't changed, golf will be hard enough, at its easiest, to be a most interesting item in the pursuit of health and happiness. Still, all the time, genius and money spent in making an excellent club are to a lamentable degree offset by not fitting the club to the player.

One of the first and most common disclosures of ignorance of the nature of the clubs to be used is seen in the way some players tee a ball for a drive.

Very few who score 80 or higher know how to tee a ball for a drive. A great many of the divots that are taken from tees by wood clubs are the result of teeing the ball improperly, rather than the result of curious efforts made to hit the ball, or even of improperly fitted drivers.

The average player tees the ball too low for the drive. The fine player tees the ball high, usually with about half of the ball being above the top of the driver when it is soled behind the ball.

The reason for this mistake is that the high-handicap man doesn't realize that the driver is made to hit the ball when the club is beginning its upswing and that the head of the club is fashioned for that particular action. The head of the driver is large to allow quite a margin of safety in hitting the shot.

Yet, most players are afraid they'll sky their drives and tee the ball low believing they'll offset their error. Their skied shots almost invariably are caused by their getting off balance while trying to throw their bodies, instead of their hands, into the shot.

When I'm teaching the drive, I have my assistant tee the first twenty balls. Then I have the pupils tee the next twenty, and every time the pupils will tee the ball about a half-inch lower until I say to them that they'll have to learn how to use a tee before they can expect to learn much about using a club.

But it must be said for the average golfer that his driver possibly has less loft than properly suits him. The driver with very little loft was a more serviceable club for the average golfer in days when fairways weren't watered than it is now. Then, a fellow could jolt a ball off the tee onto a hard fairway, and it would bounce and roll far enough to give him more distance than he should have had. Now, the watered fairways have tight and luxuriant turf. Even when fairways are mowed closer than the course superintendent believes is good for the grass, the fairway roll of most drives and wood or long iron shots is usually only a few yards.

The average player would be better off taking a brassie off the tee unless there's a strong wind against him. Against a head wind, he'd get more distance trying to bore one low into the wind than he would sailing a shot up where the head wind would cost him from fifteen to fifty yards.

Before we get away from the subject of learning how to tee a ball, always tee your ball on the short holes.

The expert has the finesse, judgment, and confidence to be justified in playing a shot from a close lie, but I have been unable to see or imagine any circumstances that would dictate that a player who can't break 80 give himself an unnecessary handicap on a tee.

Harry Vardon taught me a lesson when I was a lad and playing rounds with him. In those days, it was considered smart — possibly because there was some inconvenience in going to a box for a dab of sand — to drop the ball on the tee. That was supposed to be a mark of the expert.

I noticed that the great Vardon teed his ball on a short hole, and I asked him about it.

He replied, "I always tee the ball up if I possibly can."

Vardon had superb dexterity and finesse, so when he did not put himself to testing these qualities unnecessarily, it gave me an unforgettable example of expert thinking in making the game as easy as possible.

When Bob Jones was in the earlier stages of his development, he dropped the ball on the tee. When he became great, he teed the ball every time the rules permitted.

The top-ranking experts today all tee the ball every chance they get.

So should you. But don't get into the habit of playing "winter rules." If you do, you'll never learn to play the shots you need to be a decent golfer. "Winter rules" are generally an amusing delusion. They aid neither in the development of the turf nor of the player.

Even when the distance may be an 8-iron tee shot for the strong but not consistent player, he'd be using good common sense to take a 7-iron and tee the ball a wee bit higher. That will enable him to hit the shot without any deflection occurring from going through turf.

But again, that's a case of the player either not knowing his clubs, or not having them correctly fitted to him, or being handicapped by ignorance on both counts.

Although I am very much involved in club design and production and am fully aware of manufacturing and marketing problems, I am beginning to think that a major change in club selection for the average player may be not far in the future.

What directs my thinking is the fact that comparatively few players who score between 80 and 90 can hit an effective 2-iron or a 3-iron shot consistently. And, with the fairways as well turfed as most of them are today, there are really not many occasions when the 2- or 3-iron should have to be used instead of another club that would do the job easier and more reliably.

The size and the looks of the woods alone are psychological aids and make these clubs easier to use, by the average player, than the long irons. The irons look thinner and smaller, although they are heavier. Therefore, notwithstanding all that design genius has been able to do and despite all the emphasis of instruction, there is a chronic tendency among most players to try to lift the ball up with a long iron, instead of hitting down and letting the clubhead do the lifting.

When it's a case of using a 3-iron or a 5-wood with approximately the same degrees of loft, the 5-wood is a much easier, more dependable club for the golfer whose game is 85 or above.

I am definitely of the opinion that there is bound to be growing and well-warranted popularity of 5-, 6-, and 7-woods by the vast majority of golfers who play on courses that have fairways with any sort of turf that deserves to be called a fairway.

And let me here remind all golfers that the improvement in golf course condition, due to expert collaboration of golf course superintendents, turf scientists, and golf course equipment engineers, has considerably changed conditions for the use of golf clubs as compared to fifteen years ago.

The shafts of golf clubs have been immeasurably improved, as has every other detail of golf club design, material, and manufacture. There is one reason why this improvement hasn't been reflected in the scoring of the great majority of golfers as it has been in the scoring of the stars. That reason is failure to get properly fitted clubs.

One thing I always advise is to use a club with a shaft a little bit whippier than you might want it to be. The big idea is to have the club working for you, instead of against you.

The experts, with their strength and coordination, can make excellent use of stiff-shafted clubs for the reason that their stronger hands and arms, and their fine timing can get a lash into the shaft that the average player — even if he's quite muscular — must have provided for him mechanically.

Club designers and manufacturers go to great trouble and expense to make available clubs that will exactly fit the player. The sole of the club lies flat on the ground, and the shaft angles up toward the player so he can stand comfortably upright, with his arms hanging down naturally, and be in the most effective position for swinging and striking the ball.

This lie of the club usually is more important than the length of the shaft for, as you may have noticed, the fingertips of most men and most women, when their arms are by their sides, are fairly the same distance from the ground.

Sole Flat on Ground

With the more lofted clubs, in which precise direction and trajectory are more important factors than length, the lies and shorter shafts bring one close to the ball and make sharp-shooting easier.

Toe Slightly off Ground

On the longer irons and woods, it's not a serious fault to have the lies of the club a bit too upright so the player, when standing comfortably, may have the toe of the club slightly off the ground at address. You can "miss them

Heel Slightly off Ground

good," and get pretty fair results, when you hit the ball with the toe of the club slightly up, but you haven't a chance in a hundred to hit the ball effectively if you have the toe of the club closer to the ground than the heel of the club is when the ball is hit.

The lie and the shaft length of the putter are matters of individual preference. That preference is subject to change without notice. I've seen golfers putt marvelously well for some time, then lose mastery of the art. They'll change to some other putter, regain their knack for a while, and after going into another putting slump, change putters again and again regain the touch. We will go into further detail about that fickle implement, the putter, in the later section of this book devoted to putting.

But, on the other clubs, we'll get into definite instruction now. Comparatively few golfers completely understand the circumstances that dictate use of the respective clubs. The governing principle is to use the club that will get the ball from tee to green in the easiest, surest manner.

Here is a guide that will apply to most cases in an average player's round:

1-wood (driver) . . . From the tee into the wind, with the ball well teed-up.

2-wood (brassie) . . . From the tee with the wind and with the ball well teed-up. One reason the average golfer uses the driver off the tee, when he should use a brassie, is because the caddie hands him the driver. It's in the bag, so the boy may think the player must use it for all the shots that require a wood club off the tee. The player doesn't know any better, or forgets to think, so he takes what the caddie hands him.

The majority of players have the idea that because they may be in a fairway two hundred and fifty yards from a green, they have to use a brassie. Possibly there may be times when the lie is good enough, and the head wind strong enough to take a chance, but those times will be very few. The average player under such conditions is two shots away from the green and would be wise to take a 3- or 4-wood for his longer shot from the fairway lie and have an easy approach to get his ball close to the pin.

3-wood (spoon) . . . This is the wood club for the 85-or-higher player to use almost every time for long wood shots from good lies in the fairway.

4-wood . . . Use this club for close lies in the fairway, or for getting out of the rough when the lie isn't too heavy. This club allows a reassuring margin of error on fairway shots. Even when you almost half-top the shot, it will speed away as a good miss. When using the spoon in the rough, hit down at the ball, and it will sail away satisfactorily. If you lunge at it or try to scoop it, you will sky the shot.

2-iron . . . This is a dangerous club. Even among experts, few are reliably efficient in its use. The 2-iron's face has so little loft that it presents a mental hazard to most players. It is a murderous weapon in the hands of the few masters who do know how to use it confidently, but unless you're one of them, or want to spend a lot of time in study and practice with the 2-iron, you'd better use a wood.

3-iron . . . Much easier to use than the 2-iron. It's the longest iron that most players can use with any degree of certainty. When a 3-iron is hit well on a still day, the fellow in the 85-95 class will get approximately one hundred and sixty yards on the shot. He may try to get more distance. The impulse is to force the long irons, but the good results are obtained by hitting them easy.

4-iron . . . The average player can count on the respectable distance of one hundred and forty yards when he hits a good shot with this club. If he thinks he can get any more out of it, he's increasing his risk of fluffing the shot.

5- and 6-irons . . . There are about ten yards less distance for each higher number of iron from the 2-iron to, and including, the 9-iron. When you are using the 5- or 6-iron, you should be within easy range of the pin and should get enough elevation on the shot to have some license for banging away at the flag. The high trajectory of the shot, if hit as it should be, will keep the ball on today's soft, watered greens that hold almost any kind of a shot except the topped shot that skids over.

Figure the 5-, 6-, 7-, 8-, and 9-iron shots for less distance out of the rough than on the fairway. Then you won't be trying to force the rough shots, or gripping the club so tightly that you hack at the ball.

The 5- and 6-irons also are useful when you have chip shots that you want to have run on the green.

7-, 8-, and 9-irons . . . These clubs with pronounced lofts arc the ball up for precision approach shots. They are the finesse tools. When you know how to use them, you know how to use all the rest of the clubs.

Flanged niblick (known by various trade names) . . . This club with the wedged sole is for shots out of sand when you need loft and spin, for pitch shots over bunkers, and shots out of the rough where you don't need distance.

Putter . . . In addition to its use on the green, the putter is a most serviceable club for approaches when the apron around the green is smooth and the lie is good. It's also good for some shots out of traps bordering greens, where there are no lips on the traps and the ball can be smartly rolled through the sand, up the bank, and onto the green.

The old Scotch nomenclature of "play clubs" applied to the woods for the longer shots, and "green clubs" designated the irons. That is still a pretty sound classification of club function. The numbers of the clubs certainly don't invariably or closely determine their use.

You've got to learn where to use your clubs as well as how to use them. The expert has a tremendous advantage in that respect. You can put an 85-shooter in the same spots as Hogan, Snead, or any other star, anywhere off the green, and the expert will beat the 85-shooter from ten to fifteen strokes per round, merely by knowing the right club to use.

SIX

... Grip Holds Your
Swing Together

THE FIRST THING that determines how well you're going to be able to play is the way in which you hold the club.

The coupling between you and the club has to be right *for you*, or you haven't a chance of being able to put yourself into the shot.

I've seen some golfers become quite good despite bad grips to which they adjusted themselves by long and unnecessary practice. I've also seen some experts devise ingenious methods of holding the club to compensate for physical abnormalities. But far more than these exceptional cases, I've seen golfers who might have improved greatly absolutely destroy their chances of doing their best because they never learned how to hold the club in a physically and mechanically sound coupling of player and implement.

Innumerable times I've had golfers come to me complaining about some fault that is ruining their swings. In some instances, they'll have made their own diagnoses of the troubles. Of course, each diagnosis is as complex as it possibly can be made by the victim's profound deliberations in clinics at the club bar with others equally unqualified to analyze or instruct.

A goodly number of these victims will begin telling me what's wrong with their swings. They don't seem to realize that if they knew what was wrong, they wouldn't be coming to me and paying me for an expert diagnosis and cure.

Generally, in such cases I find that the cause of the trouble is an incorrect grip which makes it utterly impossible to get any element of the swing correct. The situations have a parallel in your own automobile. If the transmission isn't right, everything else can be O.K., but the car won't go.

When you haven't got the connection (the hands) functioning properly, your arms, elbows, shoulders, body, legs, and feet can't work in the correct manner.

The basic factor in all good golf is the grip. Get it right, and all other progress follows.

The quickest and most encouraging improvement I have been able to effect in my pupils' games has come from teaching them how to hold the club so there will be neither looseness nor dead stiffness as the ball is hit.

To hold the club properly, let the shaft lie where the fingers join the palm of the left hand. The last three fingers of the left hand are closed snugly to the grip.

A good tip is to keep the little finger of the left hand from being loosened; then the next two fingers will stay firm.

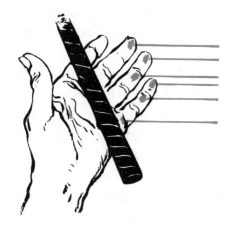

When fingers of left hand are closed properly to the grip, these are the firm points of pressure you feel.

Grip placed along roots of fingers

The left thumb is placed down the right side of the grip.

Where a mistake in the left-hand grip frequently is made is in having the shaft lie from the root of the forefinger diagonally across the palm, about to the heel of the hand.

After the club is placed at the roots of the fingers of the left hand, and the fingers closed snugly against the grip, the grip is pressed up slightly toward the heel of the hand, although it continues to lie in its original position against the left forefinger. Therefore, some make the mistake of believing that the proper placement at the beginning is diagonally across the palm.

What you always should do with the left hand grip is to keep it just as near to the roots of the fingers as possible.

The position of the left hand on the shaft definitely must be slightly over to the right of the shaft so the V of the thumb and forefinger points to the right shoulder. That's old advice, but still the best.

THE LEFT-HAND GRIP

These three fingers hold grip snugly.

The V of thumb and forefinger points to your right shoulder.

Your right hand should be put on the grip with the club lying in the channel formed when the fingers are bent, and with your left thumb fitting snugly under your right thumb.

The right little finger goes over the forefinger of your left hand, or curls around the exposed knuckle of the left forefinger. It doesn't make any difference which of these two positions the right little finger takes — whichever one you like.

THE GRIP

WITH BOTH HANDS

The V of the right thumb and forefinger also points to your right shoulder. Forefinger of right hand is against side of shaft in strongest position for hit. Hands fitted compactly together. Pressure of right-hand grip one-half that of the left-hand grip.

The right hand is placed slightly to the right of the top of the shaft.

The right thumb is in a natural position to the left of the shaft. It is important that the right thumb and forefinger be as close as comfortably possibly because these two parts of the right hand are a vital combination in a grip for power. The right thumb-forefinger combination enables you to whip the club through with all possible speed. The club is held in the right hand with about half the pressure of the left-hand grip.

Keep both hands fitted compactly together. They must coordinate the essential factors of left-hand control and right-hand power, and unless they're working closely, your hand action will be faulty.

There are occasions when a deliberate hook or slice may be required, but to play these shots with control is a job for the expert who knows just what combination of grip and stance to employ. Reducing a tendency to slice by putting the right hand more underneath the shaft is not a correction, it's a distortion. That is the method sometimes recommended (but not by me) to the chronic slicers. The opposite tendency, that of hooking, also is sometimes reduced by putting the right hand more on top of the shaft in the weaker position. Obviously, in the latter case, the more logical thing to do would be to strengthen the left-hand grip and retain the full power of the right. But, as I've previously said, failure to think simply and directly is the cause of most faults in golf.

What you are seeking and must have in your grip is the utmost effectiveness in power and control. You need to keep the face of the club in correct alignment with the path of the swing at all times, until the ball has left the clubhead.

The most serious and most frequent deviation of the clubface from its proper position occurs at the top of the swing.

What very few golfers — outside of the experts — understand is the difference between holding the club tight and not letting it get loose at the top of the swing. When I see a player hold the club tightly at address, I know that the odds are about ninety to one that the firm grip of the last three fingers of his left hand is going to open at the top of the swing, and he'll never be able to regain control of the club for his downswing.

The big idea — the essential one — is to hold the club at address with easy security rather than grim, tightening intensity. You can keep that kind of hold on the club throughout the swing. The last three fingers of the left hand hold the club firmly. The right-hand grip is relaxed, and not at all tight throughout the backswing and the early stage of the downswing. When your right-hand grip does get firmer, just before and at the moment of impact, the tightening action will be spontaneous and

The correct left-hand grip at the top of the
swing. Note how last three fingers make the
firm coupling with the club. This is absolutely
essential and must not be relaxed.

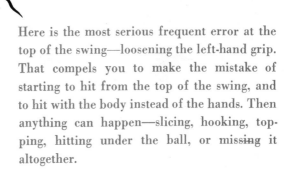

Here is the most serious frequent error at the
top of the swing—loosening the left-hand grip.
That compels you to make the mistake of
starting to hit from the top of the swing, and
to hit with the body instead of the hands. Then
anything can happen—slicing, hooking, topping, hitting under the ball, or missing it
altogether.

55

precisely timed without conscious effort. The action must take place with such lightning speed that there is no possibility of deliberate application of the muscular strength that's available in the hands.

A few very good golfers have the interlocking grip, with the little finger of the right hand entwined with the forefinger of the left, but I prefer to go with the majority

THE OVERLAPPING GRIP

The right little finger curls around the exposed knuckle of the left forefinger.

who use the overlapping grip which is called the Vardon grip. Although the great British champion wasn't the first good player to use it, he did popularize that element of golfing style in winning six British and one U. S. Open championships among his many victories.

There are several grip variations which a few of the experts use. They can get away with these deviations because of considerable practice and play, enabling them to adjust to abnormal arrangements for combining power and control. But don't try these. The unorthodox methods usually are matters of desperate experiment which ₁e experimenters don't use too long for the reason they eventually discover their golf isn't as good as it used to be.

The exceptions to standard technique which are employed once in a while by proficient players invariably are confusing to the average golfer. He may try these unusual grips which can't be used with safety, and go from bad to worse.

There isn't a first-class golfer in the world who doesn't have excellent hand action. Plainly, nobody can have a fine quality hand action without a grip ideally fitted to his kind of hands.

Golf is a game to be played with two hands. Your left guides the club and keeps the face in the desired position for the hit, and the power pours through the coupling of the right hand and the club.

Your hands must be together and work together to get the utmost leverage, balance, precision, and speed that can be applied.

Always have your mind made up that you are going to whip your right hand into the shot.

That is a "must."

Any time you hear an argument advanced against the right hand whipping into the shot, you may be sure that the objection is fallacious.

Something about the right hand that must have your thought and practice is having that part of the right forefinger, which is nearest the palm, functioning positively in the hitting action. When the right-hand grip lies firmly between the forefinger and the thumb, it is in perfect position for a fast, firm, lashing action.

THE RIGHT-HAND WHIP

The lashing action springs from the joint functioning of the forefinger and thumb.

What seems to make the left-hand position and function a mystery to some is the simple fact that the left hand, not being as conspicuous as the right hand is, doesn't get enough studious attention.

When your left hand retains control of the club as it should, you will not suffer the usual error of the higher handicap player. This is the mistake of wasting the hand action too soon.

Usually this mistake is made by straightening the wrists almost immediately after the downswing starts. Then, the ball is contacted by a stiff-arm push instead of with a vigorous whipping action.

You probably won't be able to observe in the fast action of the experts' play how their hands are over the ball or slightly past it before their wrists start to uncock. But, when you look at photographs of the stars in action, you will see how they get the right hand whip precisely at the most effective time — and much later than the average player does.

When the grip is correct, there isn't an inclination to let the right hand whip in too soon. What causes the right hand to throw from the top of the swing is that the left hand is loose, and the right hand tries to take over the function of control as well as power. Therefore, the right hand is in frantic action in a spontaneous effort to do the whole job.

By becoming acutely conscious of the necessity of a right-hand whip when the club is getting close to the ball, you will be pleasantly surprised at how your shoulders, hips, and footwork are naturally disposed to coordinate with the hand action.

There's another detail of the swing that you won't have to worry about much when your grip is correct, and that's wrist cocking. When you retain a snug grip with the last three fingers of your left hand on your backswing, your wrists are easily cocked at the top of the swing, and they're cocked in the proper, nearly horizontal plane beneath the shaft.

With a half-palm grip of the left hand, you just can't cock your wrists correctly and retain control of the club.

The uncocking of the wrists as the clubhead nears the ball is greatly facilitated — almost assured — when you have the proper grip.

In my teaching, I eliminate every possible detail that might confuse the pupil when he's actually playing. That's no time for him to be disturbed by having to make some conscious effort. He should be free from the interference of the consciousness.

I have found that one of these disturbing points is the tendency of the right elbow to get far away from the body during the swing. This fault is definitely a result of an improper grip. When the club is held correctly, the right elbow is sure to stay comfortably close to the body and pointing down. Thus does the correct grip eliminate the pupil's becoming distracted by paying attention to the elbow position during the swing. When the grip is good, that becomes good automatically.

The correct grip, which is the governing component of hand action, is certainly the greatest single detail towards achieving direction and distance of the golf shot.

When you get your grip right, you have automatically eliminated many of the bothersome details which may confuse you and prevent proper execution of shots.

CHAPTER SEVEN

How To Get Ready To Swing

BEFORE they ever begin swinging, I can improve nine out of every ten typical amateur golfers I've ever seen or taught.

At least that proportion — probably higher — have stances that don't give them a chance to do their best. They're ruined before they start.

They haven't got the dimmest notion of how to stand properly to the ball. The stance is as important as the grip. If one's right and the other's wrong, everything's wrong.

Again I emphasize the importance of properly fitted clubs. They make getting the correct stance easy.

You simply sole your club on the ground behind the ball (except, of course, in a sand trap where the rules forbid), let your arms hang comfortably, and be sure that your arms are not bent at the elbows, but extended without being stiffened. The reason for having the arms extended is to get the radius of the swing established. You'll maintain that radius when you keep your left arm extended as much as you can, without strain, throughout the swing.

The length of the shaft will determine how far from the ball you should be standing.

You will stand as upright as you can to the ball; not stiff, but comfortably upright with the knees flexed a little bit. You need to be in a natural position, without tension, so you can move without having to limber up for action while the swing is under way.

An ordinary error of players is to bend over too much at the address. Then, they straighten up as they swing, and after they've topped the ball, they think they looked up. Of course what happened is that they stood up, as they should have done at the start when they were positioning the club.

Your feet, for the wood shots, will be approximately as far apart as the width of your shoulders. For the iron shots, your feet are closer together — getting closer together as the loft of the iron increases, and the shot requires precision rather than power.

For the longer shots, the body should be facing slightly to the right of the ball instead of being parallel to the line of intended flight. For the shorter shots, your body, at address, is turned to the left somewhat, in the general direction of the hole. The amount of that turn is determined by the distance the ball is to be played. The shorter the distance, the more the body faces the hole at address.

In addressing long wood shots, the hands are even with or, in the case of the driver, just slightly behind the ball. In addressing the iron shots, the hands are slightly ahead of the ball and the shaft is slanting a bit backward to where the clubhead is soled behind the ball.

For the drive and other long wood shots, I teach a closed stance, for the long irons a square stance, and an open stance for the shorter irons.

Just in case you're not clear about square, open, and closed stances: The square stance is that which has your toes on a line parallel with the line of intended flight.

The closed stance moves the right foot a few inches back from the line with the toe turned slightly to the right.

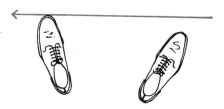

The open stance moves the right foot slightly forward of the line, and has the left foot drop slightly back of it with the left toe turned slightly to the left.

The open stance encourages a slice because it is inclined to promote a route of clubhead travel that has the face of the club coming from outside the line of intended flight in and across the ball. This gives a clockwise spin, and a slice to the ball.

The closed stance has the opposite effect. It encourages a hook.

Most golfers slice from a square stance, for reasons too numerous to mention. So, to prevent these slices and to give more distance, I teach my pupils to hit the woods from a closed stance, with the right foot two or three inches farther back than the left foot is from the flight line through the ball.

The good golfers hit their woods from slightly closed stances. The closed stance permits the hips and body to turn easily, and as much as is needed.

The primary consideration in stance and in body action is to get the body in position so the ball can be hit with greatest effectiveness by the arm and hand work.

By accenting hand action, you can avoid disconcerting thinking about any details of arm function. But you must have your body set in position to allow the arms to move naturally and gracefully.

You must have your hips in position to turn easily. Tension is set up when the hips are locked. That's what accounts for the majority of bad shots under tournament pressure. The body is prevented from moving smoothly and easily in the routine it should follow naturally.

FAULTY HIP ACTION ON THE BACKSWING

The hips are locked, and as a result the entire body is tense and awkward. If a full backswing is taken, the head will almost necessarily be pulled away from the fixed position in which it should remain throughout the swing.

PROPER HIP ACTION ON THE BACKSWING

The body is relaxed, graceful, and poised for the downswing. The head has not been pulled out of position, but the shoulders have turned properly as a result of good hip action.

A great many players turn their shoulders and think that their hip action is correct. What they don't realize is that you can turn the shoulders while keeping the hips fixed, but when you turn the hips, the shoulders go along.

When you adjust your right foot in your stance, make sure that you feel an easy looseness, but not slackness, clear up into your hip. If you neglect that, you may lock your right hip and get a sweeping slice because that rigid hip will have you bringing the club from outside the line of intended flight in and across the ball.

In your stance, the position of the ball with relation to your feet is, of course, important, but it isn't so primarily important as the distribution of your weight. About ninety per cent of all golfers scuff their shots because they haven't thought about how to distribute their weight.

In addressing your drive, have the feeling that about sixty per cent of your weight is being supported by your right foot. On the other shots, where the ball is to be hit on the down stroke or at the very bottom of the swing arc, you should feel that at address about sixty per cent of your weight is being supported by your left foot.

The sixty per cent figure is arbitrary. I don't know exactly what the percentage figure should be, but I do know that there must be very distinctly a feeling of more weight on the right foot in addressing the drive, and on the left foot with the other shots.

You don't need to worry about the weight distribution during the rest of the swing if you have taken the right stance, kept yourself in unfrozen balance, and have allowed your feet to work on the ground with freedom, but always with secure footing.

Probably more explanation is needed to impress you with the necessity of having the weight favor the left foot at address and at contact on the iron shots.

To hit a good iron shot, your club must contact the ball before the sole of the club gets to the bottom of its arc. This gets backspin on the ball, eliminates hitting behind the ball, and gets the hands ahead of the ball as the shot is hit. Having the weight borne more on the left foot than on the right as you're coming into the ball is the way of getting the correct downward path of the iron.

That combination of elements accounts for turf being taken after the well-hit iron shot is played. The club reaches the lowest point of its travel beneath the ball, rather than at the back of the ball.

The majority of players hit their iron shots badly because they are afraid of hitting down and letting the clubface go down through the ball and forward. So, these players keep their weight back on the right leg and try to scoop the ball up. That's the cause of most topped iron shots and plowing up the turf before the ball is hit.

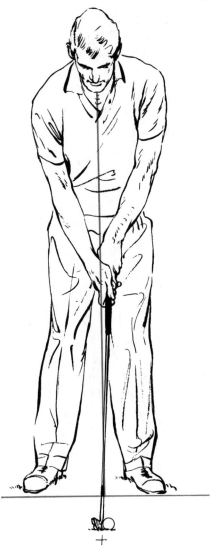

In addressing an iron shot, be sure your weight favors your left foot rather than your right foot. (See illustration on next page.)

IMPACT ON THE LONG IRON SHOT

Head is steady.

Hands are ahead
of ball.

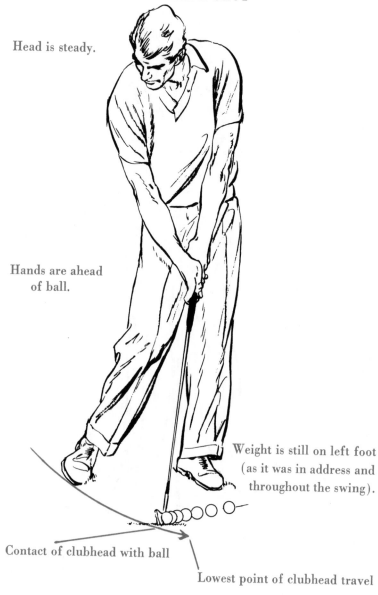

Weight is still on left foot
(as it was in address and
throughout the swing).

Contact of clubhead with ball

Lowest point of clubhead travel

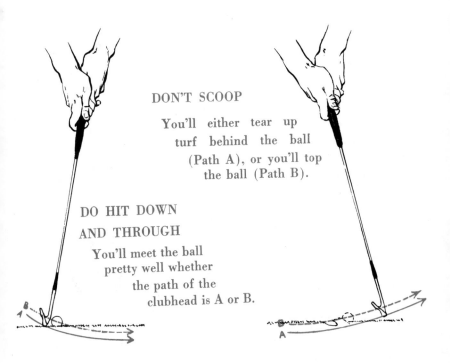

DON'T SCOOP

You'll either tear up
turf behind the ball
(Path A), or you'll top
the ball (Path B).

DO HIT DOWN
AND THROUGH

You'll meet the ball
pretty well whether
the path of the
clubhead is A or B.

You will see frequent evidence of this error as you notice that most of the 80-and-up players fall back out of balance on iron shots. They also fall forward on the wood shots. The reverse faults of losing balance would be less serious on the respective shots.

I have my pupils spend considerably more time with the irons than with the woods. When they handle the irons reasonably well, learning how to play the woods is much easier.

BALL, FEET, AND HANDS AT ADDRESS

THE DRIVE
Ball about opposite left heel
Slightly closed stance
Weight slightly on right foot
Hands slightly behind ball

FAIRWAY WOOD SHOTS
Ball about an inch behind the left heel
Square stance
Weight slightly on left foot
Hands above, or slightly in front of ball

LONG IRON SHOTS.
Ball equidistant between feet
Square stance
Weight slightly on left foot
Hands ahead of ball

PITCH SHOTS
Ball just ahead of right heel
Open stance
Weight slightly on left foot
Hands ahead of ball

CHIP SHOTS
Ball equidistant between feet
Square stance
Weight slightly on left foot
Hands ahead of ball

Note that the feet come closer together, and the ball comes closer to the feet, as the shot to be played becomes shorter.

Driving is the last thing I teach. It's the easiest part of the game. The main thing in driving is to get length. Accuracy isn't nearly so important as it is with the iron shots. Again I'll remind you that you can miss a drive and have a chance to make up for it, but you can't miss a short iron to the green without the miss costing you a stroke.

As to the position of the ball with relation to the feet:

For the drives, the ball should be about in a line even with the left heel.

For the brassie, spoon, and 4-wood, the ball should be an inch or so farther back of that line.

In playing the irons up to the chip and pitch shots, have the ball about equidistant between the feet. As the feet are closer together on the iron shots, the ball actually isn't played much farther back than on the wood shots.

The pitch shot is played from a line just a little ahead of the right heel. On the chip shot the ball is about equidistant between the feet. The swing is substantially the same for all shots, being governed in length mainly by the extent of body turn, but the different types of iron and wood shots required are determined by weight distribution and placing of the ball with relation to the feet.

With that in mind, the average player is very much inclined to study the type of shot he desires to make, instead of just stepping up and hacking away carelessly.

On the longer irons, I teach playing from a square stance with the feet slightly closer together than for the

THE ADDRESS FOR THE DRIVE

Right shoulder
   lower than left

Body facing
   slightly to the
   right of the ball

Hands slightly
   behind the ball

About sixty
   per cent of the
   weight on the
   right foot

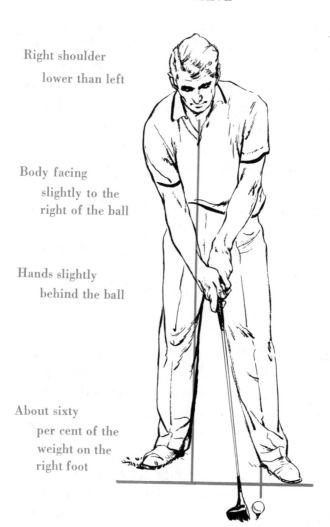

Stance slightly closed,
   with toes pointed out a bit

Ball opposite left heel
   and well teed-up

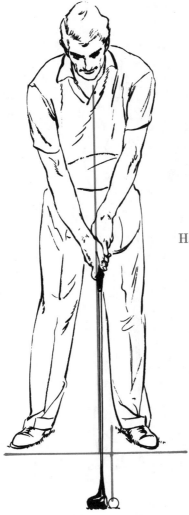

Hands over, or slightly
ahead of the ball

About sixty per cent
of the weight on
the left foot

Ball an inch or two back
from left heel

Square stance

THE ADDRESS FOR LONG IRONS

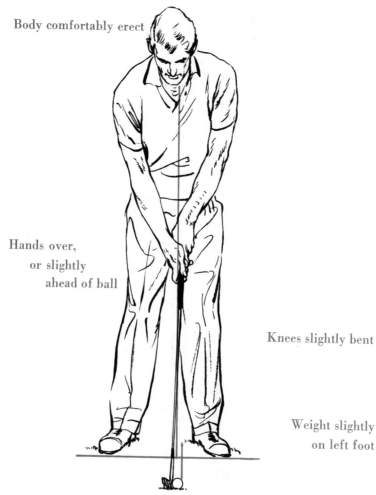

Body comfortably erect

Hands over,
or slightly
ahead of ball

Knees slightly bent

Weight slightly
on left foot

Square stance with
toes pointed out a bit

Ball back from left heel,
almost equidistant
between feet

Hands ahead of ball

Knees slightly bent

Weight slightly
on left foot

Open stance

Ball a little
ahead of right heel

THE ADDRESS FOR THE CHIP SHOT

Hands ahead of ball

Feet close together

Weight a little
on left foot

Ball about
equidistant between feet

Square stance

drive because the shot that should be played is just a little bit of a hook, or a straight ball. The long iron is being played for the green, and you don't have the comparatively large target area that warrants the distance-increasing greater hook you get from a wood played from a close stance.

The shorter irons call for less body action. Hence, the stance can be more open and the feet closer together. This stance helps you to keep from swaying, yet it permits just enough freedom to make sure that body action won't be stiff and awkward.

These shorter shots are chiefly hand and arm jobs. With the open stance promoting an outside-in path of the clubhead, the ball is given a smart left-to-right and backspin revolution that tends to give it a pronounced bite when it hits the green.

The cardinal principle of all golf shot-making is that if you move your head, you ruin body action.

Your head is the apex of the triangle of your stance. There can be slight sways that, due to foot and leg action, may move the head slightly to the right, but never out of the same triangular relationship to the legs as in address. A very few experts can do that and get away with it. But that little bit of a tipping of the triangle is highly dangerous to the average player.

The steady head assures you the balance you must have to allow your body to move properly. When your body moves in the correct way, you can do the required work of whipping the club through with the arms and hands.

What the average player does is to try to hit the ball with eighty per cent body heave. He stiff-arms the ball and makes it impossible to get needed speed of the club-head. That is the result, principally, of not keeping the head steady.

No other item of the volumes of golf advice given by the unknowing to the unsuspecting has been as fallacious as the urging to "keep your eye on the ball." You can move your head far more than enough to ruin your chance of playing a shot successfully, and yet continue to be looking at the ball.

Get your feet and your head properly set at address and keep them in the same relative positions throughout the swing, and you've got to the core of good golf.

CHAPTER EIGHT

Footwork, the Foundation of Best Golf

IN ALL athletics, good footwork is vital to satisfactory performance. Athletes are built from the ground up.

Ty Cobb in baseball, Fred Perry in tennis, and Joe Platak in handball are three whose high standing as authorities in their respective sports is acknowledged without question. Each has a magnificent playing record, and each is a profound scholar of the sport in which he starred.

I've talked to them for hours about the techniques essential to championship performance in their sports, and, without exception, they have asserted that excellent footwork is absolutely fundamental. Most certainly, this is true in golf. Without good footwork, you can't begin to achieve any proficiency near to your scoring possibilities in golf, even if you are a superbly good putter.

What prevents many ever learning correct footwork is the fact that they don't understand its purpose.

The function of correct footwork is to get the body in the right place for the arms and hands to act with maximum precision and power, and with smoothness.

A great deal of needless confusion in teaching and learning footwork arises from the fact that the subject really is so simple that people just can't readily believe that there isn't a mysterious and complicated trick to it.

So, what generally happens is a complete reversal of logic; the player endeavors to make his body work his feet, instead of having his feet impel and direct the proper body action.

In simplifying footwork, I'll give you one simple little tip that probably will greatly improve the hitting portion of your swing. The tip is to have the right knee come in fast at the right time.

Perhaps you'll think that this tip is out of order at this place, but everything else is secondary to hitting the ball, and if that right knee comes in fast at the right time, you'll hit the ball pretty well. The body, arms, and hands will coordinate with the knee action more than you realize is possible.

There's so much said that really isn't too important about the backswing. I've seen some backswings that, because of individual physical characteristics, didn't look ideally orthodox, but those backswings had two features performed perfectly. The footwork was right, and the head was kept steady.

If you're an older golfer, you'll remember how the critics used to say Bob Jones' swing was faulty because he had quite a loop at the top. You also may recall that Hagen's sway was declared by those specious critics as being a violent offense against classic form.

But all those critics missed the plot, and that was that the foot action of Jones and Hagen always got them into position to hit superb shots. The situation hasn't changed a bit today; good footwork is what makes the great golfers stand up.

If footwork is eliminated, and the player hits shots flat-footed, the club can't possibly go through in the required route. There's no power to the shot, either. The flat-footed golfer is like the fighter who hits flat-footed and can't break an egg with his punch.

Your knees are a reliable index to correct footwork.

On the backswing, the left knee moves until it is pointing to a point not too far behind the ball.

The left knee is moved into this position by raising the left heel and getting a bit of a push from the inside of the sole of the left foot, but although those foot actions are the motivating elements, they are details I seldom mention when I'm teaching as I want to avoid all possible details. I have the pupils consider knee position as the indicator of proper footwork. When the left knee is in the position it should be at the top of the backswing, the footwork has been performed correctly.

There's only one way to have the left foot function in getting the knee into the desired position, so if the pupil thinks of the result he must get, he doesn't need to worry about the details of cause.

Too often a player merely bends his left knee forward, or out. Here, for example, the knee is pointing to a spot well in front of the ball. The whole idea of knee action is lost, because unless the left knee bends in toward the ball, the hips remain stationary.

The left knee has bent in and is pointing just behind the ball. This has automatically seen to it that the hips and shoulders have pivoted correctly.

You hear and read a great deal that probably confuses you about "hitting against the straight left side," and about having the hips in a line somewhat facing the hole as the ball is hit.

If I wanted to be maliciously and deliberately confusing, I could write a long book about just those two details, but it wouldn't be understood, applied, or of any value whatsoever to any more than possibly fifty golfers in the whole world.

To boil down all that such a book would mean, practically, to the other millions of golfers, I'll say that the key to hitting against the straight left side and having the body facing as it should at impact is the action of the right knee.

When the right knee comes in toward the direction you're hitting, your right heel comes off the ground, and you're pushing the body around into perfect position for hitting. Your left side is bound to straighten up as your left knee straightens.

But, if you keep your right heel on the ground, it is physically impossible to get your right knee to play its proper part in the swing. Therefore, your entire right side — the right shoulder and the right hip — can't get into position for hitting.

The knee action in a good golf swing is practically identical with knee action in throwing a baseball.

The side that delivers the power — the right side — is

put into position to deliver by correct footwork, and only by correct footwork can this position be attained.

There's a lot of confusion about how and when to get the left heel on the ground at the start of the downswing, but there needn't be. As the right side springs into action from the right foot up, the left heel will simultaneously go to the ground.

One of my pupils — a noted doctor — came to me before we'd gone to the tee for the first lesson saying that for fifteen years he'd had the pernicious habit of pulling his left foot away from the ball every time he made a shot.

I'd never seen him hit a ball before, but I told him that I could cure him of that harmful action without leaving the locker-room. "All you have to do," I told him, "is to let the right side come into the shot by moving the right knee around toward the ball, and when you do that, you can't move your left foot out of position."

When he went out to hit some balls, he got the right knee helping with the shot instead of thinking about a negative matter of controlling the fault of the left foot, and he was cured. I didn't even mention footwork to him. Again, I must say that the greatest difficulty with footwork is that it's made bewildering by those who don't recognize its natural and fundamental simplicity.

The effect of proper footwork sometimes is misinterpreted by players who are such unusually gifted golfers they don't clearly discern the treasure nature has bestowed upon them. I've heard and read these gloriously

The right knee has bent in toward the ball, the right heel is off the ground, and the body is now in proper position for powerful hitting with the hands.

The flat-footed position of the right heel and the failure to bend the right knee in toward the ball have resulted in a body position from which no effective hit can be made.

natural golfers say they are aware of a strong pull of their left arm as they're developing their hitting procedure. They state the effect, not the cause. The cause is footwork.

What happens to them is that the right side comes from the ground up, positively at the ball, the left arm is extended, and they instinctively resist the temptation to hit too soon, hence they feel a bit of a tension which they interpret as a pull by the left arm.

It is a delight to watch the footwork of a star golfer, and particularly the work of the right foot and right knee on the downswing.

That footwork may be too quick for you to watch closely, but if you'll just watch the stars' knees, you will see the plainest, surest signs of correct footwork. The way the right knee comes in and straightens with a precisely timed action is one of the most impressive and important phases of fine mechanics in the golf swing.

But, you'll see very good action, also, as you observe an imitative youngster who's been around good players. If the kid has a good grip so he can control a club that is too heavy for him, he will move his body around by excellent footwork, and when he's making his downswing will almost be forced by the heavy club to get his body into position for whipping action of his arms and hands.

All this will mean that subconsciously and naturally, the lad's right heel will come off the ground and his right knee will bend into the shot in the correct way.

CHAPTER NINE

The Waggle, Preliminary Swing in Miniature

THE waggle, which to most of the uninformed appears to be merely an expression of nervousness or indecision, is one of the very important parts of a successful attack upon the game.

What the waggle amounts to, visually and mechanically, is the preliminary movements of the club before the backswing begins. Physically and mentally, it's much more. It gets motion started smoothly, without any jerkiness or stiffness of muscles or the necessity of exploding one's poise with a sudden start.

George Duncan once told me that a man will swing as he waggles, and I've observed that Duncan's statement is invariably confirmed. If a fellow has a fast, spasmodic waggle, he will have a fast and jerky swing. If he has a waggle of medium tempo and flexibility, without looseness, you'll see a good swing.

Cultivate a smooth waggle for, as the old Scotch saying goes, "As ye waggle so shall ye swing."

The definite purpose of the waggle is to get the muscles relaxed, and to give you a positive advantage in shot-making that you wouldn't have if you were to start from a frozen position.

There's another decided advantage of the waggle. It gives you an opportunity to check up on the feeling of your grip. The waggle is to a surprisingly large degree the hand action of the swing in miniature.

Still another benefit that you will reap from a proper waggle is the habit of studious deliberation, instead of simply an awkward tardiness in getting moving. You get time to do your thinking about the swing when it should be done — before the swing starts. You can make whatever last adjustments may be required (if any) before the club starts back, when it's too late.

It's a common experience of the average player to stand up to the ball and be on the verge of beginning his swing, when he suddenly realizes something is wrong with his stance or his grip. He will say after he's misplayed the shot, "I didn't feel right, but I just couldn't make myself step away and start all over the right way." If he'd had the habit of correctly waggling before beginning his swing, he would have been able to get the essentials attended to properly.

You see preliminary actions of a nature similar to golf's waggle when you watch good players in other sports. Baseball's good hitters pump their bats with their hands in preparing to meet the pitch. The receiver in tennis doesn't stay still as he prepares to receive the serve, but keeps moving slightly. The muscles must be loose in condition for instant and accurate response.

Great golfers have spent quite a little time in developing good waggles. They've coordinated their conscious and subconscious actions in a preliminary routine that is far beyond being only a mannerism. It is a carefully worked-out part of their games.

A fault common to many nearly good golfers is that of putting the clubhead down behind the ball after a fairly good job of waggling has been done, then letting the club stay there two or three seconds. This destroys the benefit of the waggle and means that the player actually is beginning again from a dead start.

When the waggle is completed, the backswing should be started without delay.

You can easily test this short section on the highly valuable function of the waggle by taking a club now and noticing how you impulsively waggle it. The action will be so nearly identical to the character of your entire swing, you are bound to be impressed with the fact that in improving your waggle, you'll be improving your swing.

CHAPTER TEN

The Art of Hitting with the Hands

WHEN YOU'VE got the necessary elementary though adequate understanding of how to hold the club, how to stand to the ball, and how to get into action from the ground up, the stage is set mentally and physically for the Big Show to go on.

The Big Show is a performance in the fine art of hitting.

Whether you or anybody else calls the pay-off a hit or a swing, I don't care. That's only a matter of terminology. The action is that of whipping the clubhead through the ball with the hands. Not slapping it, waving it, flinging it, stiff-arming it, but whipping it with a tigerish lash.

The great hitters in golf are those who move their hands faster than those whose distance and precision are inferior. That also is the case in sports other than golf. A fighter accomplishes knockouts by having his fists move with devastating speed. Ruth's home-run record was set during seasons when the liveliness of the ball varied, but because The Babe's hands moved faster than those of any other batter, he was supreme as a long hitter. When Jimmy Thomson was consistently the longest driver in golf, motion pictures showed his hands moving at amazing speed.

To let you in on one of the great secrets of good golf, which really isn't a secret at all, one golfer gets more distance because he uses his hands for power, while the other fellow is trying to get distance by using his body.

The long hitter gets his body in position so his hands can work most effectively.

The science of hitting in golf is a matter of a formula involving velocity and mass. The mass of the clubs varies only very few ounces, but the velocity of the hits differs tremendously among golfers. From the scientific viewpoint, a volume could be written about the physics of golf, but the practical application of such information would be limited since hitting a golf ball is more of an art than a science. It's the human element that makes the performance an art.

What misleads people into thinking that swinging and hitting are different is principally a matter of the player's temperament. Macdonald Smith and Byron Nelson have been generally identified as swingers because of the graceful appearance of their actions. Hagen and Sarazen were labelled hitters because their common characteristic was to wield their clubs with what appeared to be violent and impetuous slashing.

But, all four of them — and every other great player — had the clubhead coming in with all the speed they could command while retaining steady balance of their bodies.

Hitting the ball a long way isn't a matter of size or

weight of the player. It depends on effective use of the hands, rather than on trying to throw the weight of the body into the shot or even, within reasonable limits, lengthening the backswing in the belief that a longer backswing will enable one to accelerate clubhead speed more and get the clubhead moving at maximum speed at contact with the ball.

I was teaching a girl, five feet two inches tall and weighing one hundred ten pounds, who has become one of the junior champions. By whipping her hands at the ball and keeping her body from interfering with attainment of superlative speed of the hands, she was regularly hitting the ball at least two hundred yards.

Over from an adjoining practice tee came a former All-American football player, a huge man and in remarkably fine physical condition in his middle age. He asked if he could watch the youngster, and she blithely assented. After he'd seen her whack a dozen balls to and past the two hundred-yard marker, without seemingly undue exertion, he went back to his own tee and called to his caddie.

"Wrap up the clubs, I'm quitting," he said in disgust and walked off the tee.

Later, I saw him standing disconsolately at the bar, setting a new course record on Daiquiris.

"That child you were teaching has driven me out of golf," he said to me. "I could lift her with one hand and throw her twenty feet, but I've been taking lessons and practicing five days a week for five years, and I can't come near to hitting a ball as far as she does. I'm through."

"You can't be that hopeless. Come on out tomorrow morning, and I'll manage to get a few minutes and look you over and see if there's something that can be done for you," I suggested.

When he did come to me the next morning, I saw that he had a good-looking, grooved swing.

"Now, just hold on with the left and give the ball a good belt with the right hand," I advised him.

He turned to me, puzzled.

"Why I've always been told that golf is a left-handed game," he said.

"Give the ball a good belt with the right hand," I repeated.

He did, and to his utter amazement and jubilation, the drive carried two hundred yards.

In less than a minute, I had given him the lesson that made golf a happy game for him.

That quick lesson probably is just what most of the readers of this book need. It is:

Hold the club firmly with the last three fingers of the left hand (as I told you in the chapter on the grip), let the left arm and hand act as a guide and whack the hell out of the ball with the right hand.

On your long shots, hit the ball with the right hand

just as hard as you can while keeping the body steady, and on the shorter iron shots, hit with the right hand briskly and then, too, keep the body steady.

The reason for keeping the body steady is plain, if you'll stop and think. You can reason it out in the following logical steps:

You know you must have clubhead speed to make the ball move far.

Your hands are holding the club; therefore, your hands are the main elements in making the clubhead move. Your body and arms could remain in fixed positions, yet your hands alone could hit the ball a crisp blow.

The faster your hands move, the faster the clubhead is going to move.

But, if your body is moving ahead, too, the relative speed of your hands will be diminished.

Therefore, to get the greatest speed of the clubhead, you must get the greatest speed of your hands, and that can't be secured unless your body is on a steadily fixed, upright axis.

Your right hand, being the human element closest to the clubhead, is the instrument located to produce the clubhead speed you want.

It all adds up to the swift-moving right hand being the source of the dynamic power.

The false idea that golf is a left-handed game for right-handed players shares with the keep-your-eye-on-the-ball idea, the guilt of wrecking the development of many potentially fairly good golfers.

The left-handed game notion grew out of failure to diagnose an error correctly. The error was in blaming the right hand for overpowering the left, when what really happened was that the left hand was too weak. That error accounted for many mistakes in golf instruction and learning, since it made weakness, rather than strength, the governing factor.

No right-handed player ever has naturally hit a golf ball with the left hand, from the very beginning of the game when some ingenious shepherd took a right-handed whack with his crook at a pebble.

There is offered as proof of the argument that golf is a left-handed game the statement that Hogan and Snead originally were left-handed players. Leaving aside the accident that they fell heirs to discarded left-handed clubs as their beginning implements, consider the logic that their left-handed starts gave them strong left hands which, when they switched to right-handed golf, provided them with firm control of the club. Naturally, then, they'd give the clubhead all the right hand they could get into the shot because they had no worries about the left hand being too weak.

And with Hogan, Snead, and every other star, it is the right-handed smash that accounts for masterly execution of the shots. Don't let anyone tell you otherwise.

Now, here's something else that is vital in good hand-work:

The more you can get your hands ahead of the clubface in the downswing, the more power you can apply with the right hand.

The late uncocking of the wrists, or the delayed hit, as you may hear the effect called, instinctively causes a decided acceleration of right hand action at the most effective period.

You don't have to think about the right hand not coming along in time to whip the ball terrifically; it will get there spontaneously.

If you'll pause to consider, you will realize that if your hands are behind the ball at impact, you can only scoop the ball up. But if your hands are in front, you've got to smash the ball with lightning speed.

You don't need to accept the preceding statement as theory. Test it in practice, either indoors or on the practice tee, and you will see how positively true it is.

As you improve in the art of hitting, you will see more plainly every day that the delayed hand action is essential to getting most out of the right-hand, swift-hitting

Hands as much ahead of clubface as possible as long as possible. Steady head and body. The right-hand smash is held back until the critical instant.

power. The application of the principle is exactly the same on wood and iron shots.

With the drives, the application is when the clubhead is slightly on the upswing, due to the ball being teed up and the weight being a little bit more on the right leg.

Hitting the brassie, spoon, or 4-wood is done in the same way that irons are hit. The weight is placed somewhat more firmly on the left foot. Get your hands ahead of the ball when you hit and hit the wood clubs down just as you would the iron shots.

The experts take turf when they're hitting fairway wood shots, unless they're finessing some shot with a method that is beyond the province of this book. What I want to teach you here are the simplest and surest ways of utilizing your capabilities to the fullest extent.

CHAPTER ELEVEN

The Pause That Means Good Timing

WHEN A bad golfer gets a good shot, there is only one explanation for the accident. He has had the luck to have his timing right.

Correct timing in all athletics calls for the maximum amount of required power applied at the right place at the right instant. Timing and coordination are synonymous in all athletics, from shot-putting and hammer throwing, in which brute strength is by far the major factor, to golf, in which speed and precision of the hitting actions far outrank mighty muscles and bulk.

To coordinate, all elements of the performance must be brought into balanced common action. Some players seem to be born with the faculty of fine coordination. They are referred to as great natural golfers, rather than as synthetic stars, for the simple and sufficient reason that the gifted ones happened to apply themselves especially to golf.

A number of these versatile and naturally talented ones quickly come to mind.

There is Bob Gardner, who, as a Yale student, was the greatest pole vaulter of his time. Gardner won the U.S. National Amateur in 1909 and 1915 and was runner-up in 1916 and 1921. Although he now plays only the intermittent golf of a businessman golfer, he still will compile some sub-par scores. Jones, Hagen, and Snead have been noted as expert shots in the field or at traps. Hagen actually was good enough at baseball to have a choice, early in his career, of playing that game professionally, rather than golf. Mildred (Babe) Zaharias set records as the greatest all-around woman athlete competition has known. Patty Berg was adept at several other sports before she began specializing in golf.

But, you may not have the gift of coordination and the heaven-sent genius to time correctly the assembly of all actions in the golf shot. Don't be despondent; your case isn't hopeless.

You can learn quite satisfactory timing when you appreciate what the objective is. You want good timing because it will produce maximum distance with economy of effort. No muscular power is wasted. Economy of movement and effort are what I always am intent on teaching. I seek to have my pupils make no unnecessary movements or to exert effort that doesn't produce the best possible results.

One very simple tip will infinitely improve the timing of most golfers. Merely pause briefly at the top of the backswing.

That is the greatest single aid I have been able to give

to eliminate the worst fault in the golf swing; that of starting to hit from the top of the swing. The hacker does this almost invariably.

You can develop during practice a habit of pausing at the top of the backswing if you will count as you swing back. Make the count be One-Two-Wait-Three. "One" and "two" are counted as you swing back. Say to yourself at the top of the swing, "Wait," then on "three," start down.

Whether you make the count fast, medium, or slow depends entirely on your temperament. The advice to swing back slowly in many cases is about the worst advice that could be given. Even the man who is naturally slow and deliberate in his actions, when reminded consciously to swing back slowly, will take the club back at an abnormally retarded rate; then, by jerking the club from the top, subconsciously will try to make up for what he feels is lost time.

The pace of the backswing varies considerably. Hogan, Hagen, and Sarazen at their greatest moved the club back swiftly. Snead has about a medium tempo in his backswing. Jones and Macdonald Smith had quite slow backswings. Undoubtedly because the backswings of Mac and Bob — those paragons of style — were slow, the unthinking believed that everybody, regardless of natural pace, should have a slow backswing.

But each of the stars I have cited had a very definite pause at the top of the backswing. As a matter of fact, all excellent hitters in golf, tennis, or baseball have a slight pause at the top of the backswing during which instant everything is still from the feet to the head.

During that pause, they are subconsciously getting into accurate focus every element of the swing that must be coordinated to produce the results of perfect timing.

When you get a chance to watch Snead, note especially how he pauses at the top of his backswing and appears

THE "WAIT" OF "ONE-TWO-WAIT-THREE"

to be drawing a precise bead on the ball. He obviously looks to be in perfect position to give the ball the full treatment before he makes the tiniest move in beginning his downswing. He isn't going to pull the trigger before the target is right in the center of the sight.

Presuming that your grip, stance, and footwork have been correct in bringing you to the top of the swing, more than half the work required in hitting a good shot has

In both of these illustrations, there is the sense of full control of all the elements which have gone into the backswing. The left knee is pointing behind the ball; the full turn of hips and shoulders has taken place; the wrists are fully cocked; the head is steady.

been done, but you can nullify a large part of the value of the earlier procedure if you get impatient at the top of the backswing.

The first disaster of impatience is to tighten you and impel you to make a sudden pounce at the ball. The difference between you and a champion at this critical stage is that the champion's timing doesn't vanish. He stays at the top long enough to get set for allowing his right knee to move into the shot at the right moment (that's the plainest signal of good footwork), and to control his hand action so his right hand will stay back but whip in swiftly at the latest possible — and most effective — time.

If you're hasty starting down, you can't get power or control. Your effort will be spent long before you get near the ball, and as you hit the ball, you are far past the stage of maximum efficiency.

There is some psychological mystery about the rushing at the top of the swing I've never been able to solve. The ball is going to stay just where it is until it is hit, so there's no valid reason for making a mad dash at it.

Possibly, that's another one of the decisive stages where fear takes command over reason in golf. In the back of his mind, the player may be fearful of making a bad shot, and he rushes to get it over with and end the suspense. If he hurries, instead of pauses, at the top of the swing, his fear is realized.

Mac Smith used to say that when he wanted to hit a

long ball, he hit it a little easier. That meant he was giving himself a little longer wait at the top of the swing to make doubly sure of his timing for, if you ever saw action pictures of Mac in what's called the hitting zone and hitting a full shot, his hands were a blur. His hands were moving too speedily to be sharply photographed.

Through long experience Smith had learned that the pause at the top of the swing was a subconscious reminder that his hands instinctively would have to move their fastest at the bottom of the swing as it was manifestly impossible to get the fastest hand action at the top after a complete stop. With his pause at the top, he prepared himself to get the fullest efficiency from accelerating clubhead speed.

So many times the gap between mediocrity and proficiency is a matter of timing; I urge, as vehemently as I can, that my pupils acquire the extraordinarily valuable habit of pacing their backswings with the One-Two-Wait-Three count, and at the top get the pause that refreshes all fond hopes of hitting a good shot.

During that critical moment, the muscular and mental essentials of a good hit have the time they need to get coordinated.

Although you may think that you are inherently somewhat lacking in grace and skill, the simple affair of waiting at the top of the backswing will improve your hitting effectiveness to a remarkable degree.

CHAPTER TWELVE

Saving Strokes with Simple Approach Shots

YOU CAN SEE fellows who don't score particularly well hit long shots occasionally, and you will see others get hot putting streaks that will bring them in with scores of 90 or so. Those accidents can happen.

But you won't often see a higher handicap player playing good approach shots from off the fringe of the green to about one hundred yards out. That is the area that separates the men from the boys. Within that radius from the cup, the average golfer is lucky if he gets one of three shots near enough to give him a reasonable chance for sinking a putt.

The player who recognizes that he needs to devote his head and hands to improving his short game sees the right route to lower scores. It is difficult to get most golfers to work on this part of the game. They want to hit the ball farther than across Texas, but they are reluctant to attend to the cultivation of skill in the department where they can offset previous poor shots.

There are two classes of golfers who brightly show the great advantages of being better than the competition in the short game. One class is that of the tournament circuit stars. The other includes the veterans who win the amateur senior tournaments. The pros master the short game because they want money. The elderly amateurs get the short game rather well polished because they have seen from years of experience that the sharpshooter within the approaching range can more than counterbalance the attack of a longer-hitting opponent.

There's no need to tell one who has played a great deal of championship golf that it's the short game that decides the contests.

Offhand, I recall such lessons Paul Runyan gave when he defeated Craig Wood on the thirty-eighth hole for the 1934 Professional Golfers' Association championship and beat Sam Snead, 8 and 7, in the 1938 P.G.A. finals. It was Runyan using his spoon as an approach club more accurately than his opponents could use their pitching and chipping clubs that accounted for the David over Goliath outcomes. And when Runyan was near the green, he was almost sure to be down in two.

Denny Shute's precision approaching defeated longer hitters in winning the 1936 P.G.A. title from Jimmy Thomson, and the 1937 pro championship from Harold "Jug" McSpaden. Johnny Revolta coming out of traps to have only short putts left is what beat me at Oklahoma City for the 1935 P.G.A. championship. And in 1952, Jim Turnesa's short game took the P.G.A. crown away from the longer-hitting Chick Harbert.

Those demonstrations of the potency of the short game in man-to-man play, and innumerable demonstrations in stroke play (such as Julius Boros' brilliant short-game performance in winning the 1952 U.S. National Open and the Tam O' Shanter World's championship) must be admitted to be completely convincing. Yet probably not one of each hundred golfers who saw these stroke-saving feats I've mentioned ever went to work on improving his own short game.

That gives you an idea of why, in my personal instruction, I have to precede the actual teaching with a lecture. And that's why I repeat the order in this book. The importance of attaining some command of the short game must be made vivid to you.

The short game accounted for the great surge of American championship golf when the youngsters who'd spent time chipping, pitching, and putting in the caddie yards of American golf clubs grew up to become playing professionals. They applied their hours of caddie practice and competition to revolutionizing the old plan of play which generally considered a shot lost between tee and green as being lost forever.

Now, the shot that's missed between tee and green is reclaimed by a precision approach and a one-putt par. Pars are made into birdies and birdies into eagles by the high standard of expert approaching.

Despite all that, the amateur of any class doesn't begin to pay due attention to approach shots. You will certainly agree with that statement when you compare the standard of approaching done by contestants in the National Amateur championship with the far more dexterous approaching done by professionals who are winning money on the tournament circuit.

Now, I hope, I have sufficiently impressed you with the necessity of emphasis on the short game so we can go into the technical fundamentals.

PLAYING THE SHORT PITCH SHOT

The short shot pitched over a bunker is the most important stroke-saving shot in the game, outside of a long putt. You can play the pitch shot onto the green easily or, by being inept, nudge it into the sand and get two more wasted strokes on your card.

This shot is usually played with a 9-iron or a flanged niblick, commonly called the wedge. The club is gripped lower down on the leather than you usually hold an iron.

The shot is played from an open stance with the feet close together. This stance makes it easier for you to stand still and play the shot with the hands. There is no body action in this shot.

The ball is played almost equidistant between the feet, but a little back towards the right foot.

In addressing and making this shot, remember what I told you about having the hands well in front of the ball.

THE ADDRESS FOR THE SHORT PITCH SHOT

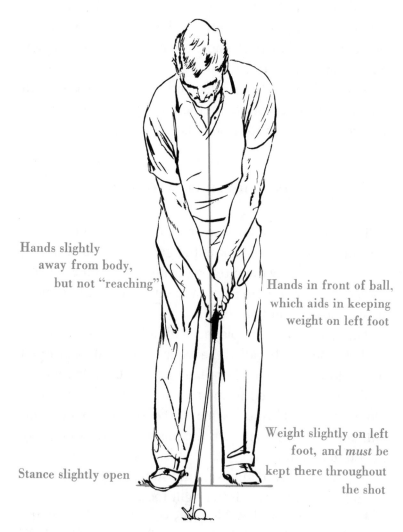

Hands slightly
away from body,
but not "reaching"

Hands in front of ball,
which aids in keeping
weight on left foot

Weight slightly on left
foot, and *must* be
kept there throughout
the shot

Stance slightly open

Ball just ahead of right heel

Feet close together

Be sure to have your weight definitely on the left foot. Your weight must not shift from there during the shot.

Often, the average player will make the mistake of not cocking his wrists enough on the pitch shot. This is a shot you have to play with a full wrist cock, although the shaft may not be taken nearly as far back as horizontal.

The club is taken back on the outside of the line and brought down with a slight inside swing which gives a high-cut shot. You don't have to pay any attention to the outside-in path of the swing; the open stance will take care of that.

Hit these short shots firmly, crisply.

Take more of a backswing than you think you may need. The ball popping up in the air will cut down distance surprisingly. Many of these shots are played so softly they go into the guarding bunker instead of going over it and falling with a bite.

When your grip is too low down on these shots, you are inclined to give the ball a push instead of hitting it. There's no back spin on that sort of a shot and when it does land, it bounces and rolls in an unpredictable way.

You probably will be wondering how to put backspin

THE TOP OF THE BACKSWING FOR THE
SHORT PITCH SHOT

Full wrist cock

Fuller backswing than you
may think necessary

Weight remaining
on left foot

Take it easy; use the
"One-Two-Wait-Three" system.

on these pitch shots. I used to wonder myself when I was taking lessons from J. H. Taylor, winner of five British Open championships, and one of the great old masters of iron play. One day I asked him:

"Mr. Taylor, how can I put backspin on a shot?"

His reply got me back to the lesson I was trying to learn. "I've been playing with you two weeks," he said, "and in that time, I haven't seen you put one ball past the pin. What you ought to be learning is how to put the ball up to the hole."

And that goes for you, too.

If you will hit down at the short pitch shot, the club will give you all the backspin you need.

This short pitch and all other precision shots are to be played without haste. The One-Two-Wait-Three count I recommended in the chapter on timing will help you to get rhythm in the approach shots.

Correct balance is essential on the short pitch, so again I say that you should have your weight mainly on the left foot and keep it there, and stand still while you're playing the shot with your hands.

I could elaborate a whole lot on this shot, but anything more would just get you into trying tricks that are beyond all but the most adroit who have fine feel, absolute control, and far more time for practicing than you can spare.

PLAYING THE CHIP SHOT

This shot from off the green when the green is open and there isn't a bunker that must be negotiated, is one shot on which the authorities have no differences of opinion.

As opposed to the short pitch shot, it's played with a square stance with the feet close together, and the ball is in a line about halfway between the feet.

The shot is played with any club that will keep the ball at a low trajectory, just so the ball will land on the green and roll without cut or hook toward the hole.

The club to be selected for the shot is determined mainly by the distance to the clipped surface of the green. The success of the experts, who can't execute the shot any better than you may be able to, is because they select the right club. Generally, they take the club with the least loft that will chip the ball onto the green and let it run toward the hole, although the lie and the amount of run desired may dictate that the adept ones choose a club of higher loft and play the ball almost off the right toe. Hold the club rather low on the grip.

You have to make sure that the ball lands on the green, instead of short where irregularities of the fairway may divert its travel from the intended line.

Keep your weight more on the left foot than the right, play the shot with the hands, and keep the body perfectly still. Have the hand action unhurried and stay down to the ball so it'll be easy for you to keep the face of the club squarely across the line and going out square to the line after the ball.

When you're playing an approach shot from the fringe of the green and your lie is good, you're better off to play the shot with your putter rather than to use any other club.

In that case, about the chief thing for you to think about is getting the ball up to the hole. If you'll keep your body still, have the club following through square to the line, and hit the ball firmly enough to overcome the drag of the longer grass of the fringe, you won't miss the hole far. You'll sink some of those approaches and un-doubtedly be playing safer than if you'd take a more lofted club and attempt a more delicate shot.

PLAYING THE BUNKER SHOTS

When the average player is in the sand that traps a green, his best bet is to try to get the ball out onto the green in one shot. But it's hard to get him to have only the modest objective of making a shot that is well within his ability. Most average players want to play the shot "cute" and hole out so they completely bewilder them-selves trying to remember a myriad of complicating factors and misplay an easy shot.

Therefore, all I tell my pupils until they're advanced players is how to play a bunker shot under normal conditions with the ball lying clean. Many thousands of words could be written about playing bunker shots under especially difficult conditions or in varying consistencies of sand, but experience and practice can do that teaching job so much better than words; we'll content ourselves with concisely presenting the fundamental points.

The shot is played with the flanged niblick, a heavy, short-shafted club with a wide flange on its sole to permit the club to slide through the sand under the ball rather than to dig into the sand.

THE BUNKER SHOT

ADDRESS

Hands a little ahead
of clubhead

Weight favoring
left foot

Clubhead not grounded

Ball a little back
from left heel

Stance open

Experts, by using that club as it is designed to be used, have eliminated one of golf's most exacting tests of superb skill, but the ordinary golfer hasn't shared in this advantage, usually because he refuses to let the club do its big share of the work.

Every outstanding specialist in the bunker shot plays the shot with practically no movement of body or knees. It's an arm and hand shot.

THE BUNKER SHOT
TOP OF
BACKSWING

Full wrist cock

Very little body turn
or knee movement

Feet flat and solid on the sand

THE BUNKER SHOT
ENTERING THE
HITTING AREA

Head steady

Maintaining the wrist cock

Very little knee action

The shot is played with an open stance which, of course, means that you'll have an outside-in swing. As the sand, rather than the clubface, is in contact with the ball, there won't be any left to right spin on the ball as there would be on a ball hit with a cut action of the club. The bunker shot will travel toward the left. Adjust your stance accordingly. Have your hands ahead of the ball as you get into position.

The grip is the customary firm though not tight hold taken on other clubs. The best bunker players grip the club at the end of the shaft.

Arms and hands
doing all the work

Practically no
body action

Club strikes sand
behind the ball

When the shot is to be played from close to the side of the bunker where a sharp rise of the ball is required, and where the cup isn't very far away, then the bunker shot should be played off the left foot. When the rise doesn't have to be so quick and the distance is longer, then the ball should be played off the right foot.

Make the club strike the sand two or three inches behind the ball and let the club go right through.

The great bunker players never stop the club quickly

after the ball comes up, but keep it going. The common mistake of other golfers is to hack down at the ball and not follow through.

THE BUNKER SHOT FOLLOW THROUGH

Club goes clear through

Head remains steady

Minimum body and knee movement

Feet remain anchored

Keep your weight definitely forward on the left foot, but have the right foot firmly anchored in the sand, too. And be sure to keep your body still.

THE OUTSIDE-IN ARC OF THE BUNKER-SHOT SWING

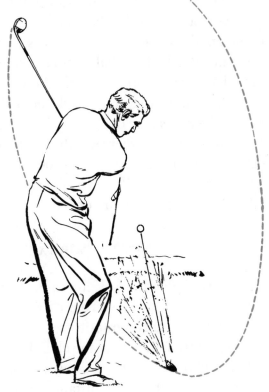

Since the ball will travel to the left, an allowance should be made in your stance so that your aim is to the right of the pin.

If the ball is in a bad lie in the bunker, don't fret. Work on it by keeping your weight a bit heavier on your left foot, take a good backswing without body movement, hit behind the ball, let the club go through and up and hope you get the ball out. You probably will.

When you have a shot in a bunker that is shallow and has no lip, there's nothing in the rules that says you can't use a putter and roll the ball out. There are times, at these traps that have no lips, when the best thing you can do is to take your putter and whack the ball briskly up the bank of the trap so the ball will drop on the green without much roll. After all, there's nothing about any club that makes its use mandatory, and if you don't use your head before you select a club, you'll make your shot more difficult and exacting than it need be.

PLAYING OUT OF FAIRWAY BUNKERS

When the ball is lying clean in a bunker flanking a fairway, take the same club you'd use for a fairway lie, unless the bank of the bunker interferes with the trajectory you may expect from the use of the club. If it does, then your club should be one that will surely get you out regardless of whatever is the most distance you can reasonably expect. The main thing is to get out.

Reduce your footwork as much as possible and whip your hands right through.

If you haven't a good lie in a bunker, take any club that will get you out on the fairway where the next shot will be easier. Where the average golfer often drops a stroke unnecessarily is by making a desperate attempt to hit a long recovery shot from a bunker and banging the ball wildly into the side of the bunker, or into a bad spot in the rough.

PLAYING SLOPING LIES

On a downhill lie through the fairway, the first thing to know is that you'll probably slice the shot, so aim the shot well to the left.

Take a slightly open stance and play the ball a bit farther back from the line off the left heel than you would play a shot from a level stance. Have your weight slightly stronger on the left foot.

As you are going to slice, you'd better take a club one or two numbers stronger than you'd play for the same distance from a level lie.

Play an uphill lie from a closed stance and allow for a slight hook by aiming to the right of the pin. Use the same club you'd use on a level fairway. Have the ball only a little bit back of the line out from your left heel and in address and all the way through have the accent of your weight on your left foot.

When you have a sidehill lie, and the ball is lower than your feet, follow the same technique as outlined on the previous page for a downhill shot. Conversely, on a side-hill lie where the ball is higher than your feet, use the

PLAYING A DOWNHILL LIE

Aim to the left
to allow for
a slice

Weight
slightly
on left
foot

Ball a little farther back
from left heel than usual

Open stance

same method of playing the shot that you would on an uphill lie.

PLAYING AN UPHILL LIE

Aim to the right to
allow for a hook

Weight
slightly
on left
foot

Ball just a shade back
from left heel

Closed stance

PLAYING OUT OF THE ROUGH

Among the details that I should mention is one little tip on getting back into the clear from the place where the average golfer often goes.

You will vastly improve your shots out of the rough if you will remember to hold the club with the normal secure grip (but only that), so that it is held firmly against the possibility of twisting.

Peculiarly enough, the two common errors in playing shots out of the rough are diametrically opposite ones. Many players let the club twist, but probably equally many hold the club too tightly. If they do the latter, this tensity spreads with the result that the main action is a heave with the body instead of a hit with the hands. This means that the ball will be hit down deeper into the rough a few disgusting yards off instead of being made to jump up and away.

CHAPTER THIRTEEN

The Fascinating, Frustrating Philosophy of Putting

THE VAGARIES of golf are never more frequently or curiously displayed than they are on the putting green.

The books, articles, ideas, techniques, experiments, hypnotism, mechanics, alleged principles, time, energy, and dreaming devoted to trying to learn and teach putting represent one of mankind's apparently endless tasks.

I have been an eager experimenter with all known theories, some of which I invented while in quest of the Great Answer. My quest continues. After all the studying with the greatest putters on both sides of the Atlantic, after countless hours of discussion, research, and thoughtful meditation, there is only one conclusion I have reached.

To become a good putter the main requisites are to keep the head dead still and make the putter blade go accurately toward the hole.

You can use any grip you like, take any stance you like, and use any putter you like. I have seen thousands of variations of putting techniques. For a while, some of the most peculiar of them hole out long, medium, and short

putts more consistently than the more orthodox methods
— if there are truly orthodox methods in putting.

There have been thousands of different types of putters
made to satisfy the blazing desire for the Magic Wand.
I know that I have bought and used hundreds of them.
After using them and winning championships with some
of them, I designed what I hoped was the perfect putter.
I am told that it is the largest-selling putter that's made
today, and I must tell the embarrassing truth that it has
been used against me to my financial loss by fellows who
have manipulated it much better than I could.

I get very hot with it, then for no reason that I can
fathom, I cool off and put my work of art away until another putter has played me false. After that I return to
my own device and find to my great joy it is true to me
again.

I won the U. S. National Open with a putter I'd got a
week before that event. A couple of weeks later, it began
disappointing me, and I gave it away.

With a wooden-headed Forgan putter that was con-
cave from heel to toe, I won the British and Canadian
National Opens, the P.G.A., and Western championships.
I thought that at last I'd found the key. But that putter
got so bad for me (not me for it) that I gave it away. Now,
I'd three-putt too many greens with a putter like that.
I've tried that style of putter again, and it simply won't
work for me.

Love and putting are mysteries for the philosophers to solve. Both subjects are beyond golfers.

But, as long as you have to get the ball into the hole, the best thing that can be done to help you is to set forth the putting problem so you can attempt to solve it in your own way. As long as hope springs eternal, you might have the answer.

Take the matter of the grip. Some maintain that the reverse overlapping gives a better putting touch. Others say there's no logical reason for changing the grip when you get on the green, as the thumb and one, two, or three fingers of the right hand are ideal for giving you just the putting touch and control of the clubface that you need.

Some putt cross-handed, finding it easier to keep the putter face accurate to the line that way.

Others have the right hand far down the shaft.

Some putt one-handed. Joe Turnesa once won the Metropolitan Open putting one-handed, after which many golfers around the New York metropolitan district began putting one-handed. Then, Joe began missing too many putts one-handed and went back to putting two-handed. The others had the same experience with that fickle art, putting, and they, too, renewed their two-handed putting endeavors.

The grips are round, oval, square, or any other shape that's legal (or illegal).

There are players who putt very well bending over

with quite short-shafted putters. Others get better results with long-shafted putters.

The heads of putters are of every shape, material and weight human ingenuity can imagine. The United States Golf Association and the Royal and Ancient Golf Club of St. Andrews have legal restrictions on the form and make of putters, seemingly in sublime optimism that someone might make a most unusual putter that would hole too many putts.

Some, when putting, play the ball off the left foot, others off the right foot, and still others anywhere in between.

One class of good putters stands with the head over the ball. Another group of good putters does well with the ball fairly far away from them.

Some are putting very well with a putter that is swung in pendulum fashion between the legs.

Others play up to the green right-handed, then putt left-handed. Opposed to this minority, there are those who play left-handed up to the green and putt right-handed.

Most players look at the ball when they're putting, but I've seen a few putt marvelously well for a time by looking at the hole as they putt.

Bobby Cruickshank went the first two rounds in a tournament with scores of 67 and 68 putting while looking at the hole, following a tip he'd received from an Australian friend. Cruicky loudly rejoiced that he'd found the answer. Then, early in the third round while putting looking at the hole, he completely missed hitting one putt. On his second trial, he hit the ball twice. It took him five putts to get into the hole on that green. End of experiment.

Now, after I've listed those contradictory features in putting, it must be dawning on you that you probably are as well qualified to work up your own best method of putting as anyone else is. About the best that the wisest professional can do for you is to give you some general pointers on putting, watch you to see what seems to work best for you, then let you practice.

When you go wrong and come back to him for a cure, he will tell you just what I've previously said, that you must keep your head still and make the putter face go accurately toward the hole.

There's other advice of a general nature I can give you about putting and that is for you to bear in mind that you usually miss the hole farther by being short or past it than you ever miss it to one side or the other. So try, in any way that you can figure out, to get your putts as nearly as humanly possible the right length.

On reading the greens, there really isn't much to be said that would be of value to ninety-nine per cent of golfers. By the time most of them finish their attempts to study the contours of a green and the nap, if any, of its turf, they haven't learned any more than a fairly well-trained caddie could have told them without delay, and they've got a few more points to confuse them and interfere with application to the essentials: direction, length, and head steadiness.

One thing, however, I can tell you is based upon my recollection of a championship when a great competitor was in favorable position, but putting badly. At lunch he asked me if I had any tips. I didn't happen to be in position to win so, naturally, I was qualified to give advice. That's golf for you.

I readily replied.

"These greens are lightning fast and sloping, so if

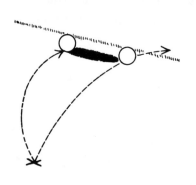

you're going to miss them, miss them on the top side of the hole," I counseled. That meant that if the slope is left to right, be sure to putt to the left side of the hole. Then the ball has a chance of dropping in from the top side, but if you miss on the low side, the ball isn't going to swerve and run uphill.

You'd be surprised if you could recall how few of your own medium or short putts are missed on the top side. That's the reason the low side of the hole is called the "amateur side."

The majority of short putts are missed by looking for imaginary slopes and hitting the ball softly, trying to "baby" it into the cup.

Confidence plays such a supreme role in putting that I am inclined to believe that if most fellows don't see the line of the putt quickly, they begin to be afraid that they will guess it wrong. The reason some great putters in professional golf look over the green with what strikes most observers as unwarranted deliberation is not that they haven't sized up the putt on first inspection, but because they want to double- and triple-check.

Some years ago, I was competing against one of the all-time great golfers. I'd holed out and walked off the green. My opponent's putt was no longer than three feet. He studied it from all angles for well over a minute, then stepped up and holed it.

He was confident he was going to hole that putt, but considering all that was at stake, he knew there was danger that he might miss it so he took every precaution possible.

It seems stupid to the man in the gallery that an expert should have trouble with a three-foot putt, but there have been dozens of marvelously fine players who didn't win titles because they failed to tap the ball thirty-six inches into a cup four and one-quarter inches in diameter.

I can't tell you how to make those three-footers, although I won the U. S. and British Opens with critical putts not much longer. The brilliant dean of the world's golf reporters, Bernard Darwin, wrote about the 1931 British Open that he'd never seen a putt hit so nonchalantly to win a championship as when I stroked my last putt at Carnoustie, where I nosed out José Jurado by a stroke.

"Nonchalantly?" I couldn't tell you, but my wife, who was in the gallery, says that I went up to that three and one-half foot putt, laid the putter behind the ball, changed my grip from the putting grip I'd used on every other green of the championship, stiffened up and rolled the ball into the hole. I don't recall seeing the putter hit the ball.

"Nonchalance" or almost paralyzed by terror?

The terrifying thought of playing with consummate skill to within a few feet of the hole, then having all previous achievement nullified by what happens within a few inches is enough to give the best golfers the yips.

Maybe there's something about mob psychology that adversely affects tournament putting. Everybody in the gallery will look at wood and iron shots and concede that he isn't nearly as good as the tournament player. But when the tournament player misses a short putt, almost every spectator says to himself, "What a dog he is; I could have made that one myself easily."

Of course he couldn't, under the same circumstances.

The golfer who I think is the greatest of them all — Ben Hogan — missed a putt of about three feet on the seventy-second green at Canterbury which would have tied him for the 1946 U. S. National Open. He didn't come close to the hole. Herman Barron also missed tying on the same green and although he was about seven feet away, his putt didn't at any time look as if it might go in. On the same green in the same championship, Nelson was short on a seven-foot putt that would have won him the title that eventually went to Lloyd Mangrum after a play-off with Nelson and Victor Ghezzi.

Another, and amazing, illustration of the pressure of circumstances in putting involves a very good friend of mine in San Francisco. He is an excellent putter. We were discussing the putt of six feet that Ralph Guldahl failed to hole at North Shore to miss tying Johnny Goodman for the 1933 U. S. National Open championship. That happened to be an extremely difficult side-hill putt, but people thought only of the distance.

My friend bet me a quite substantial sum that he could sink a putt of the length Guldahl had missed. He wanted to go right out to the eighteenth green of the San Francisco Golf Club and settle the wager.

I said we'd wait; there was no hurry. I wanted to give him plenty of time to think it over.

"Take some time and practice, if you like," I suggested, thus further reminding him of the importance of the putt.

Then I sent for a tape measure.

When we went to the green, he wanted to place the ball at a point he thought was six feet from the cup.

"Oh, no, we must measure exactly," I told him. "But you can have the ball anywhere on the green, just so it is exactly six feet from the rim of the cup. Now, you tell me what side of the hole you want to putt from." After he'd told me, I measured and very carefully placed the ball.

Following those preliminaries, that splendid, confident and opulent putter missed the cup by six inches.

He was irate. "I'll putt ten times for the same amount from the same place," he said.

"Oh, no; Guldahl had just one chance," I reminded him. He got the moral.

Everything's been tried, but nobody has been able to escape the penalty of original sin in putting. The margin of error is so tiny. If your putter is a sixteenth of an inch off line, the angle of deviation projected to the distance the putt is to be made will mean that you will miss the hole by several inches.

There's just no way to make the hole look bigger. One time Harry Cooper had a pair of glasses that made the hole look elliptical. He putted well wearing them one round. The next time I saw him, he wasn't wearing these special glasses. He told me that after he looked through the glasses long enough, the hole ceased to appear elliptical.

Now, what are you going to do with a phase of golf that is tantalizing, yet which calls for half of the strokes of par? The dub has his moments when he's better at putting than the star. There was an elderly woman in Australia who confined her golf to putting, and she'd beat the best of them at it. She defeated Hagen in a putting contest. Mark Harris, an old gentleman who was an uncanny putter and wrote a book on it, never played golf until after he had become a wizard at putting, and even then he played only a few nine-hole rounds.

You have to get for yourself some method that not only brings a very high degree of accuracy, but which will also minimize the shaking and freezing of nervousness when the pressure is on. Like many another, I've been in some tight spots apart from golf where the danger and the possible loss was infinitely greater than any that could be associated with putting. Yet, I've had more difficulty in controlling my nervous reactions in putting, and I was one of the better putters during my tournament career. I am a better putter now because it doesn't mean so much to me. The conditions aren't so severe as they were in championship competition.

How can I explain that? I can't.

How can I teach anybody to be a better putter? I can't, other than to tell them it all depends on having the putter go accurately on the line to the hole and keeping the head still.

The only additional and probably valuable advice I can give is to suggest that each golfer work out putting in his own way by adopting the method of Walter Travis, one of the most uniformly accurate putters the game has seen. Part of his practice was to putt from twenty to twenty-five feet away and have the balls come within a radius of three feet from the cup. A goodly percentage of those long putts would drop in.

Most of his practice was on putts from two to six feet. He would begin by placing four balls on each side of the hole, two feet away from the hole. Meticulously, he'd putt those four in. If he missed one, he started all over.

Then, he'd move out to the three-foot circle and place the four balls north, east, west, and south of the cup. He'd putt those in but, again, if he missed any of them, he'd begin all over.

The same procedure was followed on the four-, five-, and six-foot circles.

That's a much better way of learning and practicing putting than putting a half-dozen balls alongside each other, then tapping them at the hole.

CHAPTER FOURTEEN

Assembling Your Game in Good Order

WHEN you know the fundamentals of grip, stance, footwork, handwork and timing, the one important thing that remains for you to learn is over-all knowledge of how to assemble your game.

That, in effect, means making organized use of what you know.

Every good player steps up to a shot knowing exactly how he's going to hit the ball.

He makes his plan in advance, as opposed to the duffer who stands at the ball in a fog and then goes through motions without a definite routine.

I've often thought that if the 95-shooter would study his game as much as I have to study it while I'm giving him a lesson, he would be scoring regularly in the 80's, notwithstanding his physical limitations.

Learning yourself comes along with learning golf. There are some things that you can't do — or at least can't do often enough to depend upon them. That's the case with all of us. Your best golf may not be as good as my best golf. My best three-cushions billiards is considerably inferior to the game of Willie Hoppe, but that hasn't discouraged me from becoming pretty fair at three cushions. I know my limitations at it and play with those limitations governing my type of game.

Play within your capabilities. That means not trying to force a shot to get more distance or, in the approaches, not depending on having the absolute precision of the masters.

It will amaze you how far a golf ball will go when it is hit squarely. If you can learn that and strive for hitting the ball soundly instead of hurling yourself at it with whatever strength you happen to have, you are well on the way to lengthening your shots and making them more accurate.

Carelessness, mainly, is the cause of the majority of the average golfer's missed shots. After you've read this book, which contains the most concise basic training I know how to give — and which gives the positions and motions that have improved the games of thousands — you know what you ought to do. And what I've set forth is well within the capabilities of any golfer, male or female, of any age between twelve and seventy-two.

Your job now is to fit what you know about golf to a simple routine. You must have system. You shouldn't start changing your grip to make it right after you've taken your stance.

Arrange an order in studying the shot to be played, selecting the club and holding the club properly; then in an orderly manner to take your stance as I have instructed. Then attend to the footwork and handwork in the correct timing I have explained to you.

After that — and only after that — are you in good shape to let nature take its course.

You hear much about the value of concentration in golf. That concentration means merely the faculty of keeping the routine intact and protected against the disturbances of imagination, hazy thinking, outside influences or strained attempts *not* to do something that is faulty.

Think what to DO. That's concentration in golf.

It has been said that it helps to be stupid in playing golf. That cynical observation is far wide of the mark, although there are some excellent golfers who are not mental giants as the term is customarily used. But in giving them their just due, it must be said that their minds are disciplined to good golf, either by nature, long training to make positions and actions habitually rather than deliberately correct, or arduous work in controlling their thinking so they'll think straight when they have to and let the subconscious do the job it is best fitted to do.

You can think many good shots in advance when you understand what you are required to do and attend to the necessary fundamentals in simple good order.

What prevents many golfers from doing their best is worrying about something they've heard as a great tip.

They have heard, for instance, about "taking the club away in one piece." Like a lot of other things about golf, they aren't sure exactly what that means. It means keeping the left arm and the shaft of the club as nearly in line as possible, as far as possible on the backswing.

Maybe that will work for you. But it wasn't necessary to Hagen and Sarazen who broke the club up very sharply and soon on the backswing and certainly didn't demonstrate that failure to "take the club away in one piece" is a fatal fault.

Or you may have in mind, as you begin to swing, the oft-repeated advice to drag the club back. That has contributed lamentably to golf delinquency by encouraging sloppy grips. I suppose that the advice to "take the club away in one piece" was inspired by the sin of the advice to drag.

Get the grip I've given to you and do your footwork as you've been told, keeping your head steady, and you don't need to burden your mind with the "one piece" detail.

You may have heard confusing talk about rolling on the feet. Just how to do it you're not sure. Well, forget it in assembling your game in the simplest, most easily followed order.

See that your left knee points to behind the ball when

you swing back, and comes in pointing toward the hole as you hit, and you will have the right footwork you need. Many golfers — probably including you — can't get the club back because they don't turn their hips. They try to do tricks with their hips and shoulders when the simple footwork I have told them would be the solution of their problem.

Another detail that often interferes with lithe action is intense conscious effort to keep a straight left arm. You want to have the left arm as straight as you can without making it ramrod stiff, but the correct grip and stance will attend to most of that job.

When you have the left arm extended, you get a wider arc to your swing, the clubhead travels a little farther and puts you in position for more acceleration by the hands when you're hitting. The extended left arm also protects you against a hinging action at the elbow that will change the arc of the swing and give you an unnecessary detail for which you've got to compensate and must adjust somewhere during your swing.

Another point you may be thinking of in a way that can disorganize simple routine is that of turning the chin away from the ball at address, then hitting past it. What started that idea was a Bob Jones' mannerism. Jones turned his head to the right, like a robin drawing a left-eye bead on a worm, when he started his swing.

That mannerism got many men writing and talking

about the "master eye," and that added another confusing detail that is easily and safely avoided simply by keeping the head steady.

"Vanity of vanities . . . all is vanity"; the words of the Preacher, the son of David, come back from my childhood days at Kirk, as I consider golf instruction. Confusion of confusions, all is confusion, could be said of a great deal of golf instruction. And let me make it plain that the confusion is not the result of instruction by the competent professionals. It comes from the eagerness of unqualified tyros to give advice, plus the words of those who capitalize on the readiness of the uninformed to believe that golf is an abstruse affair with secrets deeply concealed, instead of a fundamentally simple game for human enjoyment and health.

To bring the hopeful out of the wilderness, I have endeavored to show that building one's best golf is basically a matter of laying one little essential brick of fact on top of another. I don't want to go into the chemical analysis and method of construction of the bricks and mortar, the strains and stresses on each brick, and the place of the brick in building a skyscraper.

That's for the 100-shooting amateur to teach the pro. Incidentally one of the factors that makes it impossible for a number of qualified pros to teach effectively is allowing the pupil to act too frequently as though he were the teacher.

But to get back to the brick-laying; one of the first

things I always have to contend with in unteaching pupils is to get them to organize their grips properly. After they learn that the club is taken away on the backswing with the left hand holding the club much more firmly than the right hand, they'll take the club back along the line as it should go. When they have the right hand too tight at the start, they are disposed to pick the club up and make no body turn at all.

By organizing the first thing first, the confusion about the cock of the wrists generally is cleared away. The wrists must be broken to the fullest extent at the top of the swing without loosening the left hand. The correct grip takes care of that. Where the wrists start to cock isn't of much importance if they are fully cocked at the top.

Still another detail that confuses is properly taken care of if the grip is right. That detail is the position of the right elbow at the top of the swing.

We all know that the right elbow should be kept comfortably close to the body at the top of the swing. If the hands are close together and otherwise in the proper position on the grip, you won't have to concern yourself about the right elbow being out of position.

Hundreds of times pupils are disturbed about a detail and tell me they have trouble getting the left hip out of the way. If the right side gets in as it should, the left side must get out of the way. It can't stay locked and allow the proper functioning of the right side.

Get the right knee in as I've told you, and the left side will cause you no trouble. That readily observed and easily activated right knee — the indicator of good footwork in the downswing — also takes care of the trouble of those who say they stop on the shot and can't follow-through. They stop because the right side is locked, and it wouldn't be if the right knee came in toward the ball.

Get the right knee in, keep the head still, and whip the club through with your right hand, are the main things you need to do to get a good shot.

About confusing details of all shots, I could write a dozen books larger than this one. But the job here is to teach you the fundamentals and to get you to assemble them so the details are reduced to the smallest possible extent.

You apply the basic training I've given you in this book — and at a small fraction of what I'd have to charge you to tell it to you in person — and you'll be playing the best golf that is within your command.

I know you will because the instruction has improved the scoring of thousands who now are playing much better than they ever thought was possible — and even almost as good as they fondly hope they might be able to play. It's impossible to teach you to play as well as you hope you'll play because you'll never work on your golf as hard as you hope at it. But now you'll know what you should do, and that's already a great improvement for you.

THE SIMPLE ROUTINE of an ORDERLY GOLF SHOT

1. Study the shot to be played, particularly in relationship to your capabilities.

2. Select the right club (and tee the ball correctly if it's a tee shot).

3. Take the correct grip.

4. Take the correct stance for the shot to be played.

5. Keep your head steady.

6. See that your left knee points behind the ball on the backswing.

7. Have your wrists broken to the fullest extent at the top of the backswing, without loosening the left hand. The right hand grip is firm, but not tight.

8. Pause at the top of the swing.

9. Don't rush as you start down, but get your right knee in toward the ball.

10. Keep your head steady.

11. Keep your hands ahead of the clubhead by keeping your wrists cocked, and whip your right hand into the shot at the last second.

12. Keep your head steady.

ABOUT THE AUTHOR

BORN IN *Edinburgh, Scotland, and educated at the University there, like all British boys of his generation Tommy Armour left school to fight in the First World War.*

He joined the Royal Scots as a machine gunner and later became an officer in the then new branch of the service, the Tanks Corps. While serving with the tanks he was caught in a mustard gas attack and lost his eyesight, but later he regained sight in his right eye.

The winner of many amateur golf events in Europe as well as the French Open, Armour came to the United States soon after the war ended and turned professional in 1925. In 1927 he won the U.S. Open Championship and the Canadian Open. Subsequently he went on to win every major championship: the British Open; the P.G.A.; the Western; the Metropolitan; and too many cash-prize tournaments to attempt to list.

In 1929 he took over the post of golf professional at the Boca Raton Club, in Florida, where over the next quarter of a century his instruction ranged from teaching duffers how to break 100 to brushing up the games of the top tournament professionals when they couldn't iron out their own difficulties. Armour always claimed that the instructional part of his golf career was the best—the part he enjoyed the most.